Coffee with *Jesus*

Craig F. Harrison

ISBN 979-8-89345-883-1 (paperback)
ISBN 979-8-89345-889-3 (digital)

Copyright © 2024 by Craig F. Harrison

All rights reserved. No part of this publication may be reproduced, distributed, or transmitted in any form or by any means, including photocopying, recording, or other electronic or mechanical methods without the prior written permission of the publisher. For permission requests, solicit the publisher via the address below.

Christian Faith Publishing
832 Park Avenue
Meadville, PA 16335
www.christianfaithpublishing.com

Printed in the United States of America

When you are led into the dark and it's hard to see any light, God sends people to you to lead you to Jesus. That was the inspiration for *Coffee with Jesus*, and these are the people, even though the list is long (and could be longer), that helped me to the light:

> In Memory
> Mom, Dad, Rick, Nancy, Jeff

Susan Harrison Reed, my Sister

My Children:

Roy Keenan
Rudy & Harmony Negrete
Bill & Alicia Menta
Mark & Marcie Shockley
Greg & Barbie Gerow
Jose Martinez
Herculano Garcia
Juan & Daisy Torres
Jason Gallardo
Benny & Lucretia & Joey Ruiz
Arturo & Linda Garcia

My Grandchildren:

Herky IV, Jake, Grace. Rosita, Abigail Harrison, Craig, Wyatt, Zoe, Jack Grace, Alexander, CJ, Ava, Giuli, Josiah, Jayden, Alexander, Teresa

And in Alphabetical Order

Dr. Wafeek Abdou
Dink & Mary Allen
Dr. Bill Altmiller
Steve & Kari Anderson
Carlos & Kathy Angelini
Fred & Barbara Ansolabehere
The Antongiovanni Families
Lewis & Chris Averill
Bob & Evie Ayers

Tim Bachman
Ralph Bailey
Sandy Bakich
Martha Ball
Josephine Banducci
Herman Baretto
Patricia Barnett
Sr. Hilda Silva Barrera
Diane Barrett
Sandra Bays
Bob & Andi Beechinor Family
Colleen Bellue
Betina & Gary Belter
Dominic & Edith Bianco
David Blaine
Lynn Blystone Family
George & Jen Borba
Don & Joanne Border
Gene & Mugs Borel
Bronny Bowman
Tracy & Wes Bradford
Butch Bradford
David & Lillian Brust
Anne & Brian Busacca
John & Kim Busby
Javier & Laurie Bustamonte
Jim & Bev Camp
Joe & Jana Campbell
Pat & Mike Campbell
Byron & Carol Campbell
Judy Caratan
Kyle & Kim Carter
Darren Caskey Family

Tim & Linka Chapman
Rose Cinquemani
Nick & Joann Cioppi
Jim & Evie Clark
Mike & Stacy Clarksean
John Coleman
Sean & Oleta Collins
Eric & Erica Coronado
Kathy Cota
Luis & Cecilia Cousins
Tom & Barbara Crear
Kathy & Louie Crettol
Peggy Crowe
Sang Dang Family
Natalina Davis
Deanna DeBondt
Davida Delis
Rosemary DeMarco
Brent & Anna Dezember
Sam Digilio
Sue & Russell Dixon
Fr. Larry Doersching
DeAn Drakos
Bo Durns
Craig & Lisa Edmondson
Sr. Elaine Elgart
Mike Etcheverry Family
Ron Fanucci Family
Sue & Mark Felton
Joan & Jeff Finch
Sharon & Scott Ford
Francis, my dog
Andrew Frausto
Elizabeth Frausto
Ron & Dan Froelich
Msgr. Steve Frost
John & Molly Gamboni
Kelly & Brad Giggy
Barry Goldner
Shannon Grove

Kelli & Phil Gruztka
Fran & Gregg Gunner
John, Lori & Kevin Hale
Becky & John Hall (remembering Alex)
Helen Haller Family
Jana & Skip Hardy
Dan & Rachel Hargis
Scott & Loretta Hashim
Deanna Haulman
Mikie & Dan Hay
Darle Heck
Mark Holland
Don & Patti Houchin
Jody Hudson
Kyle & Collette Humphrey
Danielle Humphrey
Sr. Mary Impellizzeri
Judy Jacobs, my assistant and friend
Monica & Bill Jeffries
Mike & Jean Jenner
Craig Jensen
Margaret Johnson & Isaac
Rick & Cindy Jones
Rosalee Jorgansen
Ken & Tara Keller
Tammy Kelly
Janie Keown
Jim & Ann Kirkpatrick
Tracy & Brian Kiser
Joan Knowlden, my mentor
Kurt & Robin Kunzmann
Diane Lake
Bill & Victoria Lazzerini
Tony & Alicia Lazzerini
Tommy & Barbara Lee
Kevin & Ashley Marie Lively
Adrienne Lopes
Conway & Elizabeth Lopez
Esther Lozano

Don & Cathy Lucas
Wayne & Deanna Lugo
Dr. Joel Mack
John & Lisa Mackessy
Annette Maiorino
Ian Manfredo
Francie & Mario Marchetti
Raymonda Marquez
Rudy, Romero, Nellie
    Mesa Martinez
Pat Marvulli
The Kevin McCarthy Family
(remembering Bert)
Dan & Vicky McCurdy
Kay Meek
George & Cindy Meek
Pat & Peggy Mellon
Sandee Menge
Diana & Tom Mestmaker
Mike & Michelle Ming
Chris & Gloria Minor
Ray Mish
Trudy Mooney
Tom Moore
Francis & Elaine Moore
Richard Morales Family
Sr. Judy Morasci
Jose Negrete
Tom & Jeannie Nelson
Nancy Wheeler Nichols
Ceciia Nichols
Mike & Nancy Olcott
Mel & Diana Owens
Kevin & Laura Pascoe
Dr. Ravi Patel
Leanne & Peyton Patrick
Barbara Patrick
Jackie Peck
Albert & Liz Peinado
Martin & Dinah Pequeno

Ken Peters
Vince & Meggan Phillips
Matt Pichardo
Toni, Tommy & Harry Placenti
Rusty Plank
Joseph Plant
Patsy & Kurt Poeschel
Jenny & David Poncetta
Don & Vivian Powell
Robert Price
Dan & Katy Raytis
The Reflections Committee
Patty & Tom Reis
Larry & Darlene Rhodes
Jim & Chris Riccomini
Brian & Carrie Riel
Kathy & John Ritter
Darrell & Shari Roberts
Art Rodriguez
Frances Rosales
Marlene & Joe Ryan
The Oscar Sablan Family
John Sacco Family
Kathy Sack
Beto & Sylvia Sala
Raji Sanghera
Cindy Schoorl
Jon & Julie Schuetz
Margaret & Don Schulte
Jim & Robin Scott
Heidi Scott
Darlene, Roylene, Jolene See
The George Serban Family
Shawn & Teri Shambaugh
Pat & Karen Skrable
Denise & Doc Skracic
Kevin & Tuesdy Small
Ken & Suzie Small
Brian Smith
Mark Smith

Mike & Marcie Soper
Jeff & Carol Sorrell
Sandy Souza
Jared Stephens
Cathy Stier
Helen Sujhada
Gene Tackett
Jeannie Temple
Kurt & Mindy Thomas
Ed & Sue Thomas
Jared Thompson
The Tobias Families
David & Anjie Torres
Mary & Sara Trichell
John & Roz Trino
My Tuesday morning Bible Study
Jeff & Joann Turman
Mike & Nancy Turnipseed
Genero Valdez
Pedro Valdez
Tonia Valpredo & Family
Consuelo Vargas
Vint & Kristin Varner
Mary Vasinda
Theresa Vasquez
Ken Vetter
Jenny & Robert Waguespack
Bob West
Mitch & Kristi Wetzel
Veronica White
Tor & Kelly Woelber
The Bill Wonderly Families
Cassie Wright
Andy & Kathleen Zaninovich
Andrew & Katy Zaninovich
Jim & Suzanne Zopolos
Franciscan Sisters of Atonement
    Sr. Sue & Sr. Alessandra
Priests, Deacons, Bishops (you
    know who you are)

Preface

In 2019, I experienced great trauma in my life. Having been a priest for over thirty-four years, with a family of eight adopted children and nineteen grandchildren, my life, as I knew it, suddenly stopped. I went into a deep depression. In my years in ministry, I have always been the go-to person for those suffering grief, trauma, and depression. Now I found myself in the middle of it.

I knew I needed help moving forward. My spiritual director suggested that I get up early every morning and spend some time with Jesus. It wasn't easy, but I began getting up every morning at 3:00 a.m., sitting on my front porch with a cup of coffee and writing in my journal. I would share my reflections with my spiritual director, and he suggested I post them. So from my morning ritual, arising at 3:00 a.m. to go out on my porch with my cup of coffee, came "Coffee with Jesus," a daily post.

I have continued to write reflections that are brief but poignant and that have attracted thousands of followers. This has also led to being hired as a speaker at the monthly gatherings for Reflections LLC, a nonprofit organization that was formed to inspire people to rely on the spirit of Christ to overcome all obstacles.

I then began a daily devotional on the Internet and was inspired to continue to reach people by including my daily posts in a book. *Coffee with Jesus* comes from a time of desperation and fear when all that was left was the presence of Christ. I have maintained this discipline for four years. Every day begins with coffee with Jesus!

January 1

As I sit and have my cup of coffee with Jesus, I reflect that to be a Christian today is not easy, but neither was bearing the weight of the *cross*. As followers of Jesus, we must be ministers of the *light*! So this *new year*, let us welcome *the light* with an attitude that is positive and *faith* filled.

Let's get up this morning and praise God for life and truth. This year, let us love our families more, forgive them more, and cherish all God gives us. Let's count our blessings! This year is *new*; let us send such a powerful prayer to the heavens that God will know we believe!

Happy New Year! It's going to be a *great* one, and it starts today! Ready or not, here we come, with Jesus leading the way!

January 2

As I sit and have my cup of coffee with Jesus, I am aware of His *loving presence in* this day. It begins when I wake up, with two feet on the ground. He has a plan, and I am part of it. His *words* are to be turned into my *actions*, and that's what makes every day *new*, an exciting experience. What will my attitude be today? Will it be one of bringing His positive message, His Word, to our world? Will I take His message of love and spread it?

Living in His presence and *light* means we become His actions. Will I get caught up in this world today or in his Word? Will I forgive seventy times seven or waste my energy holding on to the pain? Will I reach out and help somebody in need, or will I be holding tight on to my to-do list today? The choice is mine; every morning that He gives me is a new day! Will I serve Him and build His kingdom or my own?

Today, I begin my day with His Word, His promises, and His call to action. I only need to think about today; yesterday has passed, tomorrow will have its own problems. But today, I can focus on being His light in the world, making this the brightest of New Years! Have a great day and live in and be the *light*.

January 3

As I sit and have my cup of coffee with Jesus, I think about calmness. With the holiday season passing, we get back to a new norm, different, but a *new year*, and there is a need to be calm and peaceful.

John 14:27 says, "My peace I leave you; my peace I give you. Not as the world gives do I give to you! Do not let your hearts be troubled, nor let it be fearful."

This new year, let us live in that *peace*. Even when things don't seem to be going exactly how we had planned, let's strive to experience His peace, to stay calm and focused, to breathe, and to trust Him in all we do.

Today, I will celebrate this *new year* by staying calm and peaceful and allow His love and guidance to be my star! Have a great and calm day!

January 4

As I rush to have a cup of coffee with Jesus, I am thinking about rituals. I'm usually awake by 3:00 a.m., shower, get my coffee, do my meditations, and then write my reflection. Today I didn't wake up till six, got on a Zoom Bible study at 6:30 a.m., and started working out in the gym at 7:30 a.m. I got a call from someone asking me if I was okay, and I realized I had forgotten to do my post!

It wasn't exactly that I forgot, it's just that I threw myself off by not waking up early. So I'm taking a little break to write my reflection. Every day does not always go as you plan. When you get thrown off your routine, it is okay. I'm going to go back to my workout, and when I'm done, I will read my reflections and get myself ready for the day! I like routine. I don't like to be late, but I also know that life does not always happen the way we plan.

So today, I am going to be okay that I am out of sync. I'm not going to let it ruin my whole day; I am going to enjoy the fact that I can bring myself back to balance.

January 5

As I sit and have my cup of coffee with Jesus, I continued to reflect on the wisdom of Henri Nouwen, found in his book, *Life of the Beloved*. As much as he talks about brokenness, Nouwen also reflects on *blessings*, the blessings that come through that brokenness. Though it is not always easy to see your blessings when you feel attacked or depressed or hurt, the blessings are everywhere!

The *blessings* begin with waking up in the morning and forgetting your feelings, knowing that this *new* day is a *blessing*! We are able to thank God that we live in a home, have family that cares about us, food to eat, all are basic blessings. But we must go deeper. The Spirit moves us to see that even our trials are blessings, because they draw us closer to Jesus. God brings "Simons," like Simon of Cyrene, to walk and help us carry our crosses. If we open our eyes, we see that everything is changing, and *everything* is a *blessing*!

Have a blessed day, embracing the blessed changes!

January 6

As I sit and have my cup of coffee with Jesus, I was thinking about the *epiphany*. It's always been a special day for me since it was the day I celebrate Christmas with my family, all eight kids, wives, and nineteen grandchildren, as well as a few other friends. Some years, I see each family separately, but I miss the idea of having them all here together with me.

Epiphany is still an important day! When a person has an *epiphany*, they have an *awakening*, a manifestation of the *divine*! I feel in my own life an epiphany. Sometimes, we need to go through difficult times for our eyes to be opened. In those times, God truly becomes present, and we become aware of His love for us.

Have a great day, watching an epiphany in your own life!

January 7

As I sit and have my cup of coffee with Jesus, I was thinking of the word *waiting*. We might be waiting for a relationship or waiting for good news from a doctor's report. We might be waiting for a loved one to return home.

When God brings a time of *waiting*, sometimes, it seems like He is nonresponsive. We get anxious, and we try to fill that time of waiting, which might really be God's way of *sanctification*. We need to wait for God's timing because it is perfect; it will not disappoint us. We need to wait for God to *move*!

So today, I'm going to *patiently* wait. I am going to trust that God has a reason for everything under the sun. And while I wait, I will continue to know, love, and serve Him!

Psalm 27:14 says, "Wait for the Lord; be strong and take heart and wait for the Lord!" Have a blessed day!

January 8

As I sit and have my cup of coffee with Jesus, I was thinking about the violence in our world that we read about daily. I know in my own life when I have felt attacked at first, I felt that I need to be on the defensive, but when you *trust* in God, you know that He will bring *truth* and *justice*. This world belongs to Him, and so do we. I wonder if we will ever learn from the mistakes of the past.

So today, I'm going to *pray* for our communities and our families that we will turn to the Lord and learn to love as He loves. I am going to *consecrate* our *great* communities to the Lord. I hope you'll join me!

Have a blessed day!

January 9

As I sit and have my cup of coffee with Jesus this morning, I was thinking that if I were president, I would make this Love Your Neighbor Day. I would ask every person in the country to do a kind act, to reach out to someone in need, and to just be loving!

I would be excited to see the energy and positive gifts that would travel through every community and change the way we live. That's what Jesus would do, and I remind you that he is the King. So today, we can start by just being kinder and more loving. We need to be more respectful, more kind, and loving. This begins in the home.

Today, I am going to live Love Your Neighbor Day and invite you to join me.

Have a blessed day!

January 10

As I sit and have my cup of coffee with Jesus, I was thinking about a song that my friend, Heidi, used to sing with the choir, with Marlene playing on the piano, "All Is Well with My Soul!" Even the words are powerful, especially in times like this, when it seems there is so much disorder and confusion in the world.

Even amidst the chaos and trials of the day, if *our soul* is in the right place, all is *well*. It is most important during times that seem stressful or when things are not working out, that we realize that the Lord is there. I have found in my journey that this is so true. As long as I strive to follow Him, listen to His Word, and put my trust in Him, *all is well with my soul!*

I call today Soul Day! It's a day to make sure that *all is well* with my soul, because in the end, nothing else matters. So take a deep breath, recommit your day and your life to Christ, and know that *all is well.*

Have a blessed day!

January 11

As I sit and have my cup of coffee with Jesus on this beautiful morning, I was reflecting on a picture I have in my room that says, "Be still and know that I Am!" A very short sentence, but one that speaks to the heart. Amidst the chaos in the world and all the questions that have no answers, it is not easy to *be still*!

When we do sit still and rest in His presence, we get a better perspective. We know that everything is going to be okay! We become one with the great I Am! When we are still, He can speak to our heart, and He reminds us that we are His beloved. Just like when Jesus came up from His baptism, the skies opened, and they heard, "This is My beloved son." When we sit in the presence of the great I Am, we, too, are reminded that we are *beloved, blessed* that we will be *broken* so we can be *given*.

So today, find time to be *still*, sit with the great I Am, and feel the peace, the balance, the strength, and the security of being the *beloved*.

Have a blessed and beloved day!

January 12

As I sit and have my cup of coffee with Jesus, I was wondering what the greatest gift is we can *give* to each other. It's easy in times of trouble to think of what I *need* versus what do others need from me.

I think the greatest thing that we can offer, the best gift we can *give* someone, is being the best version of ourselves, offering to others *our* own inner peace, joy, love, experience of knowing Christ, and our own well-being. When we are strong and trust in Jesus, we can share that strength with others. When we live in fear or negativity, then that is all we have to offer.

Today, I am going to share the *peace* that only Christ can give. I'm going to practice living in the present moment, at peace with myself in the world as it is, and try to bring *balance* back to the universe. Just think, one person at a time, bringing the *peace* of Christ will change everything.

Have a blessed day!

January 13

As I sit and have my cup of coffee with Jesus, I was reflecting on a quote from John Henry Jowett, "God comforts us not to make us comfortable but to make us comforters." Oftentimes, God allows us to experience difficult moments and takes us to places we do not want to go or would not choose to go. He does this so that He can use us. He teaches us to *comfort* others.

Do you wonder why you've had to go through certain trials, suffering, or pain? In time, you will see God needed you to experience these things to carry out His plan. He will bring people and situations to you so that you can be the *comforter*! You will be able to share your story of suffering and how God carried you through. God will use you as a gift to others. God will use you to bring hope in times of despair. I believe there will become a time when you may even praise God for the trial; it's His Grace that has given you *true faith*!

Today, I will strive to accept God's plan and allow Him to use me as He needs! And I thank God for the *comforters* in my life!

January 14

As I sit and have my cup of coffee with Jesus, I was reflecting on a quote from St. Francis de Sales, "Do not look forward to what may happen tomorrow; the same everlasting Father who cares for you today will take care of you tomorrow and every day. Either He will shield you from suffering, or He will give you unfailing strength to bear it. Be at peace then, put aside all anxious thoughts and imaginations and say continually: the Lord is my strength and my shield; my heart has trusted in Him, and I am helped. He is not only with me but in me and I in Him."

There is so much more we can learn and so much more *peace* we can achieve if we only *listen* to the Lord. He will give us all we need for today, so forget about yesterday, and don't fret about tomorrow. Let's live today *through* Him, *with* Him, *and in* Him!

Have a blessed day serving Him!

January 15

As I sit and have my cup of coffee with Jesus, I was reflecting on a quote from St. Augustine, "God is always trying to give good things to us, but our hands are too full to receive them." So the question that we need to ask ourselves is what am I filling my hands with?

Maybe I am filling my hands with worry, wringing them daily. Am I filling my hands with busyness? Or perhaps I'm filling my hands with greed, envy, or anger. Maybe I fill my hands with violence, disrespect, or idleness. Maybe I close my hands and keep out love, grace, and peace! To receive all that God gives us, we need to greet Him with *open* hands.

Today, I'm going to let go of all the things I'm holding tightly on to and *open* my hands to the Lord! While my hands are open, I will offer Him praise and thanksgiving for all that He does and for the blessings He gives me every day. With open hands, I sing His praises.

Have a blessed day!

January 16

As I sit and have my cup of coffee with Jesus this morning, I was reflecting on the phrase, "This, too, shall pass!" I know that things sometimes seem to be getting worse. Work and family have to adjust as life changes, but one thing that is consistent is Jesus Christ!

Everything else in our life will come to an end. One problem will come and it will end, and then another one will come, and it, too, will end! The goal is to persevere in Christ, reminding ourselves daily that He is in charge. And to remind ourselves to be careful that we do not just focus on the end, but realize the real lessons come from the process. Day by day, moment by moment, lessons come for us to learn about *love*.

So today, I am ready for a *new* day. Some things today will come to pass, and others will linger, but I will hold close to Jesus Christ and enjoy the journey.

Have a blessed day!

January 17

As I sit and have my cup of coffee with Jesus, taking a day to catch up with my thoughts, I was thinking of a special verse in scripture that I call my *life* verse. When I had my conversion back in college, this scripture from Jeremiah spoke to me. Jeremiah 29:11 says, "For I know the *plans* I have for you, declares the Lord, plans to *prosper* you and not to harm you, *plans* to give you *hope* and a future."

This verse helps me to remember that God always has a plan for me, and my only responsibility is to be *open* to it. So I sit here in *gratitude* that God loves me so much and has a plan for me. Being a person who likes to have control, it reminds me how much more I must surrender.

So today, I sit in gratitude for His *plan*. I have been blessed with a beautiful family and wonderful grandkids, good friends, much support, and a deep *faith* in Christ. I don't know why sometimes I doubt there's a *plan*—He has never let me down. Today, I'm going to trust in His *plan!*

Have a blessed day!

January 18

As I sit and have my cup of coffee with Jesus on this beautiful morning, I was thinking about *strength*. What makes us strong? Usually when something difficult comes our way, a special trial or great sorrow, something that really reshapes our world, that is when we grow *strong*. When God wants to strengthen us, He allows us to enter a storm.

After the storm, we must clean up the debris, we look around, and we *rebuild*. We do things differently, too, so we will be ready for the next trial. And when we look back, we will see that the trial and separation that storm brought was needed to bring us closer to God and to become *stronger.*

Today, I am grateful for the trials, the storms, those moments when I was afraid, because they have made me stronger in my relationship with Christ. I may be battle scarred, but I have learned that it's not the *titles* we carry *but* the *testimony* that matters.

Have a blessed day. You can handle the storms when Christ is your Lord.

January 19

As I sit and have my cup of coffee with Jesus, I was thinking of one of my favorite quotes from Saint Padre Pio, "Don't worry to the point of losing your *inner* peace. Pray with perseverance, with faith, with calmness and serenity."

Sometimes, I think we forget the power of prayer. We forget that we have a gift that can lift us and our world to a better place. We may not get the answer to our prayers immediately, but God always answers our prayers. "Because God delays does not mean God denies." So pray with perseverance, with a very strong faith, and with calmness and serenity that you are being heard, that all your prayers will be answered.

Today, I am going to pray for our world, for our nation, for our community and for all of you. No one can keep us from praying!

Have a blessed day!

January 20

As I sit and have my cup of coffee with Jesus, I was thinking about two conversations I had yesterday. Both were with mothers who had lost children within the last couple of days. Listening to their pain and fear was hard, as both deaths were unexpected. I was happy they called, but sometimes, I wonder what I can do about their *pain*. I was born an enabler, and I don't like to see people suffer, but I also know that suffering is a part of life.

So I listened to them, and I wondered what someone does when they lose someone they love so much if they don't have *faith*. I do *not* want to know; it must be terrifying. Faith and time will bring some healing, but lives are changed forever. In the book I'm reading, the author talks about life and death, and he talks about what happens after we die and go home to heaven. He says the *one* who sent us on the mission is waiting for us to come home and tell the story of what we have learned. I like that! My life here is creating experiences of *love*, some easy, others painful, but all lessons. And then when I get to the other side, the Creator will ask me to share how I found Him in all of these experiences!

Today, I don't have time to waste worrying about things. I'm going to focus on the experiences of finding God in what I call today, that is *living*!

Have a blessed day!

January 21

As I sit and have my cup of coffee with Jesus, I have been thinking a lot about anxiety people can experience. I have always been a worrier, or I should say, I used to be one! I try to practice daily surrendering, surrendering my day to the Lord, asking for His guidance, and then, throughout the day, trusting in His plan.

One of my favorite quotes is from Norman Vincent Peale, "Worrying is accepting responsibility God never intended you to have!" Sometimes, we have to actively remove worry from our lives. This is where prayer comes in. We must turn to God and give God our concerns and worries. It takes practice, but the Holy Spirit will help!

So today, with everything that's going on, there is nothing to worry about because Jesus is still the King of Kings. We are God's children. God gave us Jesus, who gave His life for us, and all we have to do is trust—trust in Him!

January 22

As I sit and have my cup of coffee with Jesus, I was thinking of a reflection I read that said, "God invites us to drop our burden on Him, and unlike the dry cleaning, you don't have to pick it up again." Sometimes, we need to laugh at ourselves. We say we *trust* Jesus, we surrender our problems to Him, and if we don't see an immediate response, we pick those problems up again and we hold on to them tightly.

Surrendering is an *art* that we all must practice. It takes trust, it takes perseverance, and it takes love. Sometimes, I must surrender things ten to fifteen times a day because I keep wanting to take them back and turn them into worry.

So today, unlike the dry cleaning, I'm not going to pick those problems up. I'm going to let them go, because Jesus can handle it. He always has and always will.

Have a blessed day…and don't forget the dry cleaning!

January 23

As I sit and have my cup of coffee with Jesus, I was thinking about all of the people who have been talking to me about loneliness and depression. Both are very real things. If you're one of the lucky ones who doesn't suffer from them, know that you still play an important part in the lives of those who do.

Throughout my life, I have dealt with depression, and I've also had some times of loneliness. But I've never really felt alone. Part of that is because I'm an extrovert and I like being around people. But there are serious issues in our world today, and the scriptures offers us great help when we are feeling down or alone. One of my favorite scriptures is, "The Lord Himself goes before you and will be with you; He will never leave you or forsake you. Do not be afraid; do not be discouraged" (Deuteronomy 31:8).

So if you suffer from depression or loneliness, know you are never alone. The Lord *is* with you! If you don't suffer from depression or loneliness, know that a simple phone call, a kind word, a text can make all the difference to someone who does! Never be afraid to reach out to someone!

Have a blessed day!

January 24

As I sit and have my cup of coffee with Jesus, I was thinking more about people who suffer from depression, anxiety, and loneliness. One of the devotionals I love is "Streams of the Desert."

Yesterday, the reflections talked about Matthew 14:13, "And He withdrew...To a solitary place." Sometimes, God calls us to a solitary place. Psychologists call it depression, anxiety, or loneliness!

The devotional went on to say that certain times in our lives are like music; God creates a space for a *pause*. Those periods of time are just as important as the musical notes themselves. We have to learn, in the times of depression, anxiety, or loneliness, to embrace the *pause*; it is essential for the entire masterpiece. So maybe today, it is time to withdraw and spend some time alone with the Lord, asking yourself these questions: What is He teaching you? Where is He taking you? And what is He asking of you?

We don't have to be ashamed, embarrassed, or afraid of our moments of depression and anxiety. It is just part of the melody of our lives and an important part of the bigger picture. What's more important is it's filling our lives with the presence of the Lord! Let's enjoy all the blessings He brings during those periods of *pause*.

Today, I'm going to embrace the *pause*!

Have a blessed day!

January 25

As I sit and have my cup of coffee with Jesus, I was thinking about Sunday mornings. During the week, I like to think about preparing for them. As a child, we would get up and go to church. We dressed up and had to change clothes as soon as we came home. After that, we would have breakfast, and it was always a big breakfast. I always felt there was something *glorious* about Sunday, the Lord's Day. My dad gave us a work pass that day, meaning we didn't have to do useless chores.

I think *glorious* is a great word for Sundays. Taking time out of our day to acknowledge all that God has done for us and to *celebrate* our response to His love! Nothing gives us an excuse for not making the Lord's Day *glorious*!

So on every *glorious* Sunday, celebrate church, celebrate family, even if that means just FaceTime or a call, and celebrate a big breakfast! Celebrate His creation and all the blessings that come with it.

Take a walk, sing a song, call a friend, make your favorite dish for dinner, and in all of this, *celebrate* His *glorious* day!

January 26

As I sit and have my cup of coffee with Jesus, I am reading the scriptures. I was reminded that we cannot let ourselves be *intimidated*. The other day, a friend sent me a letter about how his high school–aged child is being bullied and how disconnected his son feels. We can all feel that way when we let people intimidate us. If Jesus is the Lord of our lives, we do not have to be intimidated by others; rather, we need to be focused on God's Word!

There are always people who will threaten us, belittle us, refuse to listen to us, or even bully us. But if we stay focused on God's Word, we have nothing to fear. People intimidate because they are lacking in the Spirit of God and are seeking power. We need to pray for them, that they may find the Spirit of God in their hearts. Everyone is broken, and the more they run from their brokenness, the more they must exert power.

So today, I am going to lift those who seek to intimidate me. I am going to pray for them, that they may experience God's love and *peace*. Today, I'm going to be *forgiving*, for this is the day the Lord has made. Let us rejoice and be glad in it.

Have a blessed day.

January 27

As I sit and have my cup of coffee with Jesus, I was thinking about one of the other gifts of the Holy Spirit, *kindness*.

Kindness is defined as the quality of being kind, generous, and considerate. Kindness is often mentioned throughout the Bible. I think it is one of the gifts of the Holy Spirit that we need to practice in the world today.

The scriptures say, "Love is patient, love is *kind*; Love does not envy or boast; It is not arrogant or rude" (1 Corinthians 13:4). And in Ephesians 4:32, it says, "Be kind and compassionate to one another, Forgiving one another, Just as in Christ God forgave you!" Can you imagine our world today if we could just be kind to one another? It begins at home, being kind to the people we live with. I challenge all of you reading this to begin practicing kindness at home, with husbands being kind to their wives, and wives being kind to their husband, by reminding children to be kind to each other, and to their parents and by being kind to our coworkers, kind in our texting, posting, in all other forms of communicating.

Today, I am going to strive to be *kind* to everyone I encounter. I will also strive to be *kind* to myself, trusting that God has a perfect plan, centered on the gifts of the Holy Spirit, one of which is *kindness*.

Have a blessed day!

January 28

As I sit and have my cup of coffee with Jesus, I was thinking about another one of the fruits of the Holy Spirit, *joy*! There is a difference between happiness and *joy*. We can be going through very difficult moments in our lives and still feel *joy*, the *joy* that Jesus is our Lord and that there is nothing to worry about.

I'm reading a book by Henri Nouwen. He states that the greatest gift that we can give anyone is our own personal inner *joy*, peace, silence, solitude, and well-being. We may want to do things for people or sometimes feel that we're taking on other people's problems and issues, otherwise known as codependency. But that does not really help them. What people need to experience is the inner peace, *joy*, and the positive energy that flows from a person who knows the Lord.

Today, I am going to focus on *joy*! Everything may not be perfect in my life, but I do feel God's presence deep within my heart, and that brings *joy*.

That is the greatest gift I can share today!

January 29

As I sit and have my cup of coffee with Jesus, I was reflecting on *timing*. Sometimes, it seems that everything in life is about *timing*.

A good comedian knows how to use timing when telling a story or joke. A good cook must rely on timing to create a wonderful meal. A good preacher knows when to stop! Even our streetlights are timed to keep us from having accidents. We have calendars, schedules, clocks, and alarms, all to help with *timing*.

I wonder how many *times* we turn to God and ask that we live in His *timing*. We need to trust that when we are called to *wait*, there is reason. When we are called to action, the *timing* is important. The scriptures tell us, "Wait for the Lord; be strong, and let your heart take courage; wait for the Lord!" (Psalm 27:14). Again we hear in Isaiah 40:31, "But they who wait for the Lord shall renew their strength; they shall mount up with wings like eagles; they shall run and not be weary; they shall walk and not faint." We read in Ecclesiastes 3:1, "For everything there is a season, and a time for every matter under heaven."

Today, I know I will look at my watch, I will check my calendar, and there will be many other ways in which I will be made aware of time. But I am going to pay special attention to God's *timing* in my life.

Have a great day and make *time* for the Lord!

January 30

As I sit and have my cup of coffee with Jesus, I was thinking about the word *enough*. In our world, it always seems like we need more, more time, or more time off, more money, or even more time to spend with God! But the reality is that God always gives us *enough*. It is what we do with that time that is the problem. To begin our day in prayer, surrender, and reflection means we must take some of the *enough* time and apply it. Sometimes, we have to say *enough* to the things we waste time on.

Every day, God provides us with what we need, and it is *enough*. My mother used to say, "Enough of that, enough worrying, enough complaining!" What she meant was that's all…move on. Just today, God is providing us with enough, enough time, enough love, enough means to be the best version of ourselves. It becomes our choice to live in enough.

So today, I'm going to live in the now, with enough. I'm going to be grateful and patient and know that enough is enough.

Have a blessed day in the knowledge that one day is enough!

January 31

As I sit and have my cup of coffee with Jesus, I was reflecting on the amazing things God does in our lives. I was thinking about my eight children. How young I was when God brought them into my life. I certainly didn't know what I was doing, when at twenty-one years of age, I got the first one. In time, I was blessed to be given the responsibility of eight, and they gave me nineteen grandchildren. Who would have thought that God had a plan for all of us, together?

It is good to go back and look at the gifts God has brought into your lives. Yes, there have been struggles and trials, but as I sit here with my cup of coffee, I feel overly *blessed*. On this cold morning, it is great to wake up and know that the *living* God has blessed and will continue to bless His *children*.

So today, pour a cup of coffee and look back and see all the ways that God has blessed you and cared for you. He is not done. If you do this, it cannot help but be a wonderful day!

February 1

As I sit and have my cup of coffee with Jesus, I was thinking of the words *connection* and *disconnection*. As I go through my day, I'm always trying to find *connections*. It may be connection with God, with friends, with what I'm reading, or who I am listening to. I need connections! I'm also aware of the things I need to *disconnect* from each day. I need to disconnect from the negativity, the gossip, and the judgment; there are even people I need to disconnect from.

What are you connecting with today and what do you need to disconnect from? Today, maybe God is calling you to connect with Him in prayer (He *always is*). Maybe it's time to connect with a family member or friend. God may also be calling you to disconnect: to disconnect from the amount of time on your cell phone or on Facebook. Maybe there's someone that you need to disconnect from because they are keeping you from being the best version of yourself.

Today, I am going to focus on connecting with our Lord. I think I may have a second cup of coffee with Him. I think today I will disconnect from the news media and maybe even the *refrigerator*! Life is about connecting and disconnecting!

Have a blessed day *connecting* to Him!

February 2

As I sit and have my cup of coffee with Jesus, I was thinking about how oftentimes, I feel like just a drop of water in the ocean. When I get caught up with the negativity of so many peoples' different ideologies and movements, some that are so mean-spirited, I get frustrated.

At times, I feel like I'm swimming upstream. But then, I hear the voice of God. He calls me to silence and teaches me to swim with the current of His grace. He teaches me to swim to a new place, ready to step foot on an island of truth and hope. God is my compass. Don't get me wrong; there are times when we also have to swim upstream against the current to do what's right. God will give us the courage and strength.

Today, I'm going to go with the flow and let God take me where He needs to take me, knowing that He guides me and directs me!

I'm going to share a poem that a friend of mine, Joan, wrote; it speaks to me!

> Drink Me…
> by Joani

> As I look around me,
> swimming in the sea,
> I wonder what happened,
> and where it will lead me.
> How did I get here when
> I believed life was stable,
> I worked so hard
> for people to be able
> to build a tighter connection
> between God I know,
> and people I see,
> the hearts that are broken,
> the pain overflowing.
> I'm reminded of Alice in Wonderland,
> who picked up a bottle that said, "Drink me,"
> and when she did, she became so small,
> her tears flowed like rivers and became the sea.
> She swam in the water of lies and deceit,
> confused with betrayal,

that safety had been promised
to her, if she was loyal.
How do I capture these tears one by one,
put them back in the jar?
I can't do it alone, God, I need your help,
This has gone too far.
with your help it has shrunk,
Not an ocean at all,
Not again will I
"Drink me,"
I'm now ten feet tall.
It's a drop.

Have a blessed day.

February 3

As I sit and have my cup of coffee with Jesus, I was thinking about a quote I read that says, "Remember...interruptions are often God's way of saying, 'Hey, I need you over here!'" I call these moments *sacred interruptions*. A *sacred interruption* is when you have your schedule and your to-do list and everything is going along well, and then you get a text or a call or an email, and God takes *you* in a different direction.

I used to fight these *sacred interruptions*, but now I realize I need them. They remind me that God is taking care of me and that, oftentimes, my plan is not His plan. Whenever this happens, I can see afterward how He was trying to get my attention because He needed me to do something for Him! I now expect them and welcome them. So today, if God blesses you with *sacred interruptions*, embrace Him and know that He is guiding you, loving you, and directing you to where you need to be.

Have a blessed day!

February 4

As I sit and have my cup of coffee with Jesus, I was thinking about the word *focus*. I was talking with one of my grandchildren who was telling me how hard it was for him to *focus* in class. Then a friend of mine called me and said he had a hard time focusing when reading the scriptures, how his mind kept wandering.

I think all of us have some brain fog which keeps us from being able to *focus*, but one thing we can *focus* on is God's *love*. Every day that we wake up, God breathes new life into us. We don't need to overthink it, we really don't have to focus on it, we just have to gratefully accept it. Yes, we may be struggling with focusing on some of the simplest things. Last night, I went downstairs, and I couldn't even remember why I went down there. I still don't! But what I am going to focus on is God's love.

So today, don't worry if you can't remember what you're doing or even why you're doing it, just remember God loves you, and when you're confused, think of Him!

Have a blessed day and focused day!

February 5

As I sit and have my cup of coffee with Jesus, I was thinking about the word *aware*. Yesterday, I sat on my porch for a little bit and threw Francis his ball. (Francis is my dog.) I started looking around, and I became *aware* of so many things. I noticed that the trees had lost their leaves, there were a lot of tangerines on my neighbors' tree, and I must confess, they are very sweet. I watched neighbors walk by, waving or stopping to say hello, others in too much of a hurry as they rushed down the street.

Awareness is something I need to practice more often. Sometimes, I can be in such a hurry or have too much on my mind that I do not see that I'm not aware of all of God's miracles happening right before me. A hummingbird just came, and I sat so still, it just stayed right in front of me. I think of all the times I missed seeing God's presence because I was in such a hurry.

So today, I am going to practice *awareness*. Awareness in the simple things, the sound of the birds, the colors in the sunset, cloud formations, and all the other gifts that God has in store for me today! Join me on Awareness Day!

Have a blessed day! (I have to go throw the ball again!)

February 6

As I sit and have my cup of coffee with Jesus, I was thinking about weekends. Even though all the days seem to run together, the weekend is a time to practice my mantra of *slow down, simplify*, and *sanctify*. It's a time to renew our *spirits*. Maybe you had a long week at work, or you were locked up in the house with the kids all week, or maybe it was just a lot of time alone. It's time to make every weekend *sacred*!

On Sacred Weekends, I challenge you to go for a walk or a bike ride, call a friend, prepare a fun meal, read a book, and maybe take a little extra time to converse with the Lord. We can take a regular day, not fill it with busyness and craziness, and allow our *spirit* to renew itself.

So let's declare every weekend a Sacred Weekend. Do something that you have been putting off that will renew your *spirit*. Take a little time by yourself with the Lord, sit in the yard and look at nature, go for a hike, or just be silent in His presence. I love Sacred Weekends.

Have a blessed day!

February 7

As I sit and have my cup of coffee with Jesus, I was thinking about a quote that someone sent me yesterday. It says, "Sometimes you have to let go of the picture of what you thought life would be like and learn to find *joy* in the story you are actually living." The quote comes from Rachel Marie Martin. It reminds me of how Jesus tells us to live in the present moment.

I don't know too many people whose lives turned out exactly as they planned. Oftentimes, things like employment, divorce, death, and so many other things change the course of our lives. But when we remember that our lives were given to us by God, we are reminded that we need to accept each and every hardship as part of our journey.

Today, I am going to strive to find the joy and blessings that God has given me. I am going to look at the things I have survived and how much deeper my relationship with Christ is because of this. Today, I am going to live in *joy*!

Have a blessed day!

February 8

As I sit and have my cup of coffee with Jesus, I was reflecting on the word *mercy*. The dictionary defines *mercy* as compassion or forgiveness shown toward someone who is within one's power to punish or harm. Throughout the Bible, the word *mercy* is often used. Jesus refers to it all the time. And I try to follow His teachings. Luke 6:36 says, "Be merciful, just as your father is merciful." Titus 3:5 says, "He saved us, not because of righteous things we have done, but because of His *mercy*." Hebrews 4:16 says, "Let us then approach God's throne of grace with confidence, so that we may receive *mercy* and find grace to help us in our time of need." One of my favorite devotions is the Divine Mercy. God shows us endless *mercy* and asks us to do the same to one another.

Today, I'm going to strive to be more *merciful*. I am going to reflect on the gift of Divine Mercy: "Jesus, I trust in you." We are so blessed to have a *merciful* God.

Have a beautiful day!

February 9

As I sit and have my cup of coffee with Jesus, I was thinking about *life*. Yesterday, my seven-year-old grandson got a Happy Meal, and in it was a miniature version of the game of Life. We played it for a couple of hours and laughed over and over again. Sometimes, we can take *life* too seriously. Instead of basking in the beauty of God's creation, the little miracles He shows us each day, we get caught up in the problems of *life*.

To truly live means to have a *life*. Every once in a while, I would say to someone, "You need to get a *life*!" But the life that God has planned for us is perfect! Sometimes, we need to just surrender and go with the flow. There will always be things that challenge us in this *life*, but when we allow Jesus in, there is nothing we cannot handle.

Today, I am going to celebrate *life*, not just my personal *life*, but the *life* of my community, the *life* of my family and friends. Today, I will celebrate *life* with gratitude and thanksgiving.

Have a blessed day!

February 10

As I sit and have my cup of coffee with Jesus, I was thinking about the word *courage*. The definition of courage is strength in the face of pain or grief. I have been blessed in my life to know many people who are *courageous*! I have a friend who is battling cancer; she's fighting the fight. I also know a young boy who is fighting that same fight with cancer. I watch them rely on their faith in God. I have friends who have lost their long-time spouses and friends who have lost children. The list goes on and on. They all continue to have a positive attitude in their pain and strive hard to be *courageous*!

Scriptures tell us in 1 Chronicles 28:20, "Be strong and courageous. Do not be afraid and do not be dismayed, for the Lord God is with you." And Psalm 31:24 says, "Be strong, and let your heart take *courage* all you who wait for the Lord!"

No matter what is happening in your life, whatever trials come your way, have courage and *trust* in the Lord. Thank you to all of you who remind me of what courage is all about!

Have a blessed day!

February 11

As I sit and have my cup of coffee with Jesus, I was thinking about the word *loss*. Later today, I am attending the funeral of a long-time friend, someone who has always felt like part of my family. In the past, I know many of you have lost family or friends as well.

I also know that grief is a part of everyday life; it is something thing we all have in common as human beings. I read a great quote that grief is just love with no place to go! I think the biggest struggle is what do we do with the *loss*. As a person of faith, I know that friends and family who have passed are okay. And sometimes I feel selfish for missing them so much. I think about the next life, and it brings me peace. But you cannot avoid the emptiness and the sadness.

So today, I'm going to allow myself to feel the loss and pain. It's not self-pity; it's just reality. I'm going to count as blessings those I've lost and be thankful for the impact they made in my life. I'm going to give thanks to God, because without experiencing loss, we can never experience gain.

Have a blessed day.

February 12

As I sit and have my cup of coffee with Jesus, I am filled with *gratitude*. What a beautiful day yesterday was. We had a wonderful send-off for a friend, and I spent time with so many friends. It was great to see so many people. It also reminded me that when things and times are difficult, *gratitude* is the answer. I realized how blessed I am. I am blessed to have a deep faith in Christ, and even with challenges, Jesus reminds me of all the things I should be *grateful* for.

I can find myself complaining about things or worrying about things that I have no control over, but in the end, I am *blessed*. When I take a deep breath and I think of all that Jesus has done for me, I can't help but be overwhelmed with *gratitude*.

So the next time you feel blue or attacked or things seem out of control, just take five minutes and count your blessings. It works every time! It's going to be a *great* day, and don't forget to be *grateful*!

Have a blessed day!

February 13

As I sit and have my cup of coffee with Jesus, I was thinking about what it means to *let go*. There are so many things we need to *let go* of! We may need to let go of hurts from the past. We may need to let go of relationships and friendships that are unhealthy. We may need to let go of held-in anger and resentment. The good thing about letting go of things is that it makes room to *hold on* to things that are important.

Today, maybe you could think about what you need to let go of. Make a list of four or five things that trouble you. Then make a list of four or five things that you want to embrace. It's amazing how the small exercise can put things into perspective. I am working on my list this morning and had to stop at four or five because I probably have fifteen things I need to let go of. But today, I'm going to pick only four or five. My list of what I need to hold on to is inspired by Jesus. I need to hold on to His love, His strength, His word, His forgiveness, and His mercy.

So today, I am calling it Selection Day. Select what needs to go and what needs to be held on to.

I guarantee it will be a wonderful day!

February 14

As I sit and have my cup of coffee with Jesus on this beautiful morning, Valentine's Day, I'm reflecting on *love*. *Love* is a word that has been misused. People say I *love* my job, or I *love* my car, but in reality, *love* is reserved for human connections (and pets). Jesus is the fulfillment of *love*! To lay down your life for someone else because of *love* is the greatest sacrifice.

So on this Valentine's Day, first and foremost, I am grateful for the *love* given to me by God. I'm also grateful for the *love* passed on to me by my parents; that love continues even though they have passed. The *love* of my children and grandchildren makes me feel like the most blessed person there is.

So today, whatever your day is going to be made of, remember the people who have shown you *love*. Those who loved you in good times and in bad, in sickness and health, give thanks to God! And don't forget to thank Him for the love He gave us sending us His son Jesus.

Have a blessed day, and happy Valentine's Day!

February 15

As I sit and have my cup of coffee with Jesus, I was thinking of the word *encourage*. Last night, I had a great talk with a couple of my sons, and I was really encouraged. Each one of them has overcome so many obstacles, and yet they continue to fight the fight to be good men, good fathers, and good Christians. The dictionary says *encourage* means to give confidence, support, or hope to someone. These special men continue to *encourage* me to press forward.

Think of the people who have *encouraged* you in your life. The teachers, the coaches, the parents, the ministers, the bosses, all of those who taught you how to be a better person. It's funny for me that God has brought eight young people into my life forty years ago and that they now range in age from fifty-three to forty! I realize they have encouraged me more than anyone. I have always felt Jesus encourage me, speak to me, and guide me, and He has done so by bringing many people like them into my life to encourage me.

Today, I am thanking God for all those who *encourage* me along the way on my journey. A special shout-out to my sons for striving to be the best that they could be. It's inspirational!

Have a blessed day!

February 16

As I sit and have my cup of coffee with Jesus, I was thinking about the word *attitude*. I believe that attitude is a state of mind. As I woke up this morning, I have to put both feet on the floor, and I tell myself this is going to be a wonderful day. Since I'm still half asleep, I sometimes have to repeat that a few times. But as I wake up each morning, I say, "Lord, today help me to use this day to bring joy and hope and peace to the world."

Sometimes, I wake up without having enough sleep, or something is on my mind, and I have to strive harder to have the right *attitude*. I need an *attitude* that today is all about serving God. I always have lists of things I need to accomplish, things I look forward to, and sometimes things that I dread, but my *attitude* is what matters.

So today, as I sit and have my cup of coffee with Jesus, I'm having an *attitude* of *gratitude*!

Have an amazing day and an amazing *attitude*!

February 17

As I sit and have my cup of coffee with Jesus this morning, I was thinking about *dreams*. I was talking to a friend yesterday, and she said something profound. We were talking about depression, the disconnect of the world, and she said, "I can't find the dream." It seemed like an epiphany! In this strange time we live in, when we barely remember what day it is, it seems we have forgotten how to dream. We used to dream of the future, of a vacation, or of fellowship at church. We had routines; now, it all seems different.

Perhaps Jesus is calling us to something deeper. Where we used to fill our time with busyness and activity, now there is a tremendous *void*. Perhaps Jesus is wanting to fill that void. Jesus wants to be a part of the *dream*. We can go through the motions, fill our time with useless things, or we can open our hearts to Jesus. We can allow Him to fill that void, and then we can dream again! We can dream again of greater things, greater times, greater blessings.

Today *dream*. *Dream* of a world that Jesus wants. Dream of a world of peace and joy and love. And then hold on tight because *dreams* do come true.

Have a blessed day!

February 18

As I sit and have my cup of coffee with Jesus, I was reflecting on Psalm 40:1–2, "I waited patiently for the Lord's help; then He listened to me and heard my cry. He pulled me out of a dangerous pit, out of the deadly quicksand. He set me safely on a rock and made me secure." That scripture is very powerful. Sometimes, we need to make changes in our lives, changes so that we can deepen our relationship with Christ and serve others in our greater way.

When we walk with Him, we are on the safety of the rock and are made secure. We can battle, we can spend our life fighting, or we can live for, with, and in Him! What is holding you back from following Jesus? Whatever it is, it is time to move out of the pit and into His arms. We have nothing to fear when we follow Christ!

Today, live in His presence, embrace His journey, celebrate His love, and get out of the dangerous pit, the pit of self-pity, lack of trust, worry, and anxiety! Stand securely on the rock. Have faith in Jesus!

Have a wonderful day!

February 19

As I sit and have my cup of coffee with Jesus and enjoy a beautiful Bundt cake that was left for me, I can only think about the words *thank you*. I fell asleep early last night. I was exhausted, but before I went to bed, all I could do was tell the Lord, "Thank you. Thank you, Lord, for being my strength!"

I thought of all the friends who have walked with me over years, some of which were so dark; they continually reminded me to look to the *light*. I want to *thank* the Lord for the gift of all my friends and family, my children and grandchildren who have held me up. My true friends, and I mean true friends, who have never left my side.

So today, I am grateful it is a new day. I am a new man, and God is going to be the only one who tells me what He needs me to do! I can't wait to see what today holds! Thank you to all of you who read *Coffee with Jesus*. It keeps me close to Him and to you.

Have a blessed day, and thank you!

February 20

As I sit and have my cup of coffee with Jesus, I was thinking of the word *shepherd*. I have always loved Psalm 23, "The Lord is my shepherd, there is nothing I shall want!" The dictionary defines a *shepherd* as one who tends his sheep. I am sure that is why the scriptures always refer to Jesus as the true Shepherd. If one of them goes astray, He leaves the ninety-nine and goes after the one that is lost.

When we say that the Lord is my Shepherd, we make a claim that Jesus is the Lord of our life and that it is He whom we follow. Scriptures tell us that a Shepherd knows His sheep. I find comfort knowing that Jesus knows me and that He is the one I need to follow. I find comfort that Jesus would search for me if I were lost.

So today, whatever is going on in your life, know that Jesus is the True Shepherd. He will lead you to quiet waters and refresh your soul. He will guide you and lead you on the right path for His name's sake. He will anoint your head with oil, and your cup will overflow. What more do we need? Today, I am going to rejoice in my Shepherd, Jesus Christ!

Have a blessed day!

February 21

As I sit and have my cup of coffee with Jesus this morning, I reflect on the word *change*. Everything in the world is in motion, and whether we like it or not, everything is always changing. It says in Romans 8:6, "The mind governed by the flesh is death, but the mind governed by the Spirit is *life* and *peace*." And Isaiah 40:31 says, "But those who hope in the Lord will *renew* their strength. They will soar on the wings of eagles; they will run and not grow weary; they will walk and not be faint."

When God takes you on a journey and you have to face change, embrace His Word. God does not want us to get too comfortable in this life for this life is not his promise. Jeremiah 29:11 has always been my life verse, "I know the plans I have for you, declares the Lord, plans to prosper you and not to harm you, plans to give you *hope* and a *future*." So when God takes you out of your comfort zone and brings *change* into your life, it's for His purpose. As difficult as it is, embrace it, celebrate it, and live it. Every day is Resurrection Day!

So today, look and see how God is bringing about change and don't be afraid. Get excited because the best part of your life is about to begin!

Have a blessed day!

February 22

As I sit and have my cup of coffee with Jesus, I was thinking about the word *strength*. A friend of mine sent me a reflection by Danielle Koepke. She says, "Being strong means refusing to tolerate people and things that wound your soul."

It's not always easy to be *strong*. A good question to ask ourselves is why are we afraid? Where can we get strength from? Strength comes from within. I love the Bible story of David and Goliath. Strength comes when we are centered in Christ, and we are not afraid of anything because we know He leads us.

We gain strength, and each day, we set out to do God's *will!* When we allow the God that lives within us to guide our feet, we are strong! When we are afraid, we lack trust in the promises of Christ. Scripture reminds us where our strength comes from. Nehemiah 8:10 says, "Do not grieve, for the joy of the Lord is your strength." Isaiah 41:10 says, "So do not fear, for I am with you; do not be dismayed for I am your God. I will *strengthen* you and help you; I will uphold you with my righteous right hand."

So today, greet the day with the strength of the God that lives within you. Put a smile on your face, make a difference in our world, and shine! There's nothing to be afraid of when our strength comes from God.

Have a blessed day!

February 23

As I sit and have my cup of coffee with Jesus, I was thinking about *problem-solving*. I know a lot of friends who were raised not to talk about their problems and that denial has caused even greater issues. Sometimes, we spend more time reacting to a problem than just taking care of it and solving it.

All people have problems they have to work through. We need to focus on solving our problems. Sometimes, this means setting a time frame, collecting data, or sometimes, even just letting it go. Just because we have problems does not mean that God is punishing us;

in fact, that is absurd. Problems are just a part of life; what we do with them is the real test.

So today, face and *solve* today's problems. Don't worry about yesterday's, there's nothing you can do about them. Turn to God and ask for guidance and help! It says in Philippians 4:6, "Do not be anxious about anything, but in everything by prayer and supplication with thanksgiving let your request be made known to God." Proverbs 3:5 says, "Trust in the Lord with all your heart, I do not lean on your own understanding." Matthew 7:7 says, "Ask, and it will be given to you; seek, and you will find it; knock, and it will be open to you."

Today, turn to the Lord, solve the problems at hand, and then let them go. Live in His peace and love!

Have a great day!

February 24

As I sit and have my cup of coffee with Jesus, I am thinking about the word *new*. Don't you love it when something is brand-new? The smell of a new car or when you get a new house or even new shoes. Brides and grooms always look forward to their brand-new life together (those of you who have been married over twenty years know that there are challenges they have no idea will come their way!).

One day, we will have a new earth! Jesus tells us in Revelations 21:5, that "I am making everything new!" One day, everything will be made *new*, a new heaven and a new earth. I am excited to know that I am a part of that, as are you. It's the promise of our baptism. Yes, we may have to endure suffering in this life and pain and loss, but we count on the fact that our home in heaven is going to be *brand-new*. There will be no more pain and suffering, no more tears and anguish.

Today is a *brand-new* day, and it's going to be exactly what you make out of it. So celebrate the gift of something *new*, and look around at all of the blessings you have.

Today is going to be a great *brand-new* blessed day!

February 25

As I sit and have my cup of coffee with Jesus, I am thinking about the word *trust*. There have been many times when I did not trust where God was taking me. A few years ago, I was traveling on a train in Italy. When I switched trains, I got on the wrong one. I was traveling alone, so I got very nervous. It was going to be hours before I would be able to get off, switch trains, and head back. When I sat in the section of the train I had been assigned to, I spent the next three hours making new friends. And I've kept them for life.

Sometimes, God takes us to places and puts us in situations so that we can grow, meet new people, and find connections. I now consider that train ride to be one of the greatest blessings I have received. When we let God be the conductor and lead us where we need to go, we will see that there is a reason for everything. It says in Proverbs 16:9, "In their hearts humans plan their course, but the Lord establishes their steps."

Today, go wherever the Spirit leads you, even if you don't understand. *Trust* and be patient. God may have placed you there for reasons you have no idea of. Follow the Spirit!

Have a blessed day!

February 26

As I sit and have my cup of coffee with Jesus, I am thinking about the word *perspective*. No matter how wonderful life seems to be going, if our *spirit* is crushed, it's almost impossible for us to experience *joy*!

But when our *perspective* is heaven, then we can endure almost anything! Fifty years from now, most of us will be long gone. Everything we went through on this earth will have no more meaning. The only thing that will matter is eternal life.

The scriptures tell us in Romans 8:18, "I consider that the sufferings of the present time are not worth comparing with the glory that is to be revealed to us." Everything we go through, everything that God allows us to experience, is preparing us for an eternal life in His presence!

So today, realize that all of the suffering, the pain and loss, is nothing compared to the promise of eternal life, where there will be no more suffering, no more tears or pain. Keep things in *perspective*, and today is going to be an amazing day, one day closer to being with the King of kings.

Have a blessed day!

February 27

As I sit and have my cup of coffee with Jesus, I'm thinking of the word *persevere*. There is a difference between perseverance and endurance. Perseverance consists of having absolute trust in what is going to happen. To *persevere* through hardship is built on the trust that there is nothing to fear. Jesus stood for love, peace, justice, forgiveness, and mercy.

To *persevere* means to believe in this, that we will not be let down because Jesus is always at our side. There may be moments in our lives we experience disappointment, challenges, and even suffering, but through it all, we remain faithful to God's promises. We want to be like Saint Timothy who said, "I fought the good fight. I finished the race. I kept the faith!" Today, *persevere* with joy and peace. Be a true witness that Jesus is the Lord of your life!

Have a blessed day!

February 28

As I sit and have my cup of coffee with Jesus, I was thinking of the phrase that Jesus said in Mark 4:39, "Peace; be still." Sometimes, we need to quit thinking and just be still. Sometimes, we need to just tell ourselves to be still. Everybody thinks too much and about too many things. When we're thinking all the time, it's hard to live in the present moment, and the words *peace* and *still* need to be repeated.

When we are *still*, our senses are stronger. We become more aware of the sounds of creation, the smells and the sights of miracles unfolding every moment. Saint Francis of Assisi learned this in his lifetime. It allowed him to experience God in the city, in the mountains, in creation, wherever life took him.

Just as Jesus calmed the wind and the sea with the words, "Peace, be still," He does the same with the worry, anxiety, and the frustrations we often experience. Today, repeat those words often as you go about your day. Listen to the healing words of Christ, "Peace, be still."

Have a blessed day!

March 1

As I sit and have my cup of coffee with Jesus, I was thinking of the sculptor's hands. A friend of mine, an artist in Canada, sent me some clay. I have been practicing taking this block of clay and letting God guide my hands to create! Isaiah 64:8 says, "We are the clay, and You are the potter. We are all the work of Your hands!"

I may not create a masterpiece, but that doesn't matter. Just working the clay, seeing the transformation, reminds me of what God is doing in my life. So often, I have tried to be the potter in my own life, creating an image that was not the God in me. It's like the vase that I tried to make in junior high school. When I brought it home, my mother said she loved the ashtray!

Today, we can trust the Lord to mold us, sometimes to squash us and re-form us, to become the magnificent piece of art that we are. Today, I am going to celebrate that God is still creating this masterpiece!

Have a blessed day with God as the Potter.

March 2

As I sit and have my cup of coffee with Jesus, I was thinking about the phrase, *overcoming fear*. Fear can be so debilitating. I realize that for much of my life, I have lived in fear. I was afraid of making mistakes, afraid of the dark, afraid that someone wouldn't like me.

God has led me through a wild journey from fear to trust. Today, I am not afraid! It says in Romans 8:31–32, "If God is for us, who is against us? He who did not withhold His own son, but gave Him up for all of us, will He not, with Him, also give us everything else?"

When we live in fear, we cannot live in the trust and grace of the Father. We either put our hope and trust in Him or in the world, where fear is produced. If you're tired of being afraid, afraid of people, afraid of situations in your life, or afraid of life itself, then it's time to turn back to the Father.

Today, remember that with Jesus we have nothing to fear! Jesus came here that we might have life and have it abundantly!

Have a blessed day replacing fear with trust!

March 3

As I sit and have my cup of coffee with Jesus, I was reflecting on the word *transition*. If you look it up in the dictionary, the word is defined as the process or a period of changing from one state or condition to another. We all go through transitions in our lives. Maybe you have been through a divorce, a job change, a move to a new area, or lost someone you love, all of these bring us to *transition*.

We cannot stop *transition* from happening, but we can certainly rely on Christ to help us through. It says in Joshua 1:9, "Be strong and courageous. Do not be frightened, and do not be dismayed, for the Lord your God is with you wherever you go!" And Jeremiah 29:11 says, "For I know the plans I have for you, declares the Lord, plans for welfare and not for evil, to give you a future full of hope." The scriptures are full of reminders that when we are in *transition*, we need to lean on the Lord.

So today, I'm going to see the *transitions* in my life as a true blessing and a gift from God. I will cling to Him for direction and support.

Have a great and blessed day!

March 4

As I sit and have my cup of coffee with Jesus, I was thinking about the word *excitement*. It seems like a long time since people have been *excited* about anything. The other day, a friend said to me, "The only thing I am excited about is going to bed at night and saying goodbye to a nothing day."

As Christians, we should be *excited* about many things. We should be excited about each new day and the many ways in which God speaks to us. We should be excited about God's Word and know that we're not alone. There is a plan.

So it's time to wake up and get *excited*. It's time to stop complaining about what was and be excited about what *is*. Just think, we have a whole day to see God's hand at work, and we have a choice to be *excited* or *bored*. I'm going to choose to be *excited* today!

Have a blessed and exciting day!

March 5

As I sit and have my cup of coffee with Jesus, I was thinking of the word *choice*. Every day of our lives, we make choices. I wish I could say we always make good *choices*, but that is not always true. The wonderful thing is that if we make a bad choice, we are blessed to have faith and a new chance to make things right. Today, as we wake up, we can make a *choice* as to how we're going to live. We can begin by dedicating our day to serving Christ.

We need to think often about the *choices* we make, and we need to include Jesus in them. We can *choose* to put a smile on our faces and greet people with joy, or we can be negative all day. We can *choose* to see the beauty of God's creation or we can spend the day complaining. Isn't it a wonderful gift that we get to *choose*?

Today, I'm going to *choose* to make this day a day of joy, love, and forgiveness. I am going to *choose* to put a smile on my face and celebrate a new day! What a great day to be grateful and to *choose* to make the world a better place!

Have a blessed day!

March 6

As I sit and have my cup of coffee with Jesus, I was thinking about the word *kindness*. Ephesians 4:32 says, "Be kind to one another, tenderhearted, forgiving one another, as God in Christ forgave you." Yesterday, I witnessed so many acts of *kindness*. From breakfast in the morning with a priest friend, to all the people that came up to me, to lunch at Woolgrowers, the waitress, all the people. Everywhere I went, I experienced *kindness*.

I visited a few friends who are very ill and the *kindness* their caregivers were showing was beautiful. Colossians 3:12 says, "Put on then, as God's chosen ones, holy and beloved, compassionate hearts, *kindness*, humility, meekness and patience." Can you imagine what our world would be like if we all did simple acts of *kindness*?

Today, be aware of the tone in your voice, of all of the occasions that God gives you to share *kindness*, and act on it. As we show *kindness*, we show God!

Have a blessed and kind day!

March 7

As I sit and have my cup of coffee with Jesus, I was thinking about the word *closure*. Someone sent me a quote the other day that said, "If the door *closes*, quit banging on it! Whatever was behind it wasn't meant for you. Consider the fact that maybe the door was *closed* because you were worth so much more than what was on the other side."

Throughout our lives, we have moments where there is *closure*. It could be the death of someone we love, or the end of a marriage, or a change in our occupation, or even things like depression and anxiety. Sometimes, we need to take a good look at our lives and not be afraid to *close* the door that brings pain and then open the one with new beginnings. It's amazing how many doors keep opening. I think that's how Jesus works.

Today, don't see closure as something negative but rather as something positive and exciting. I used to love the game show *Let's Make a Deal*. I always wanted to know what was behind door number 2!

Have a great day and just watch as new doors open and the Spirit of God leads you.

March 8

As I sit and have my cup of coffee with Jesus, I was thinking about *laughter*. Yesterday, we had a little celebration of life for a classmate from high school. Although he left us too early, getting together with his family and other old classmates brought lots of laughter. Even amidst our sadness, the laughter was healing.

I think it's important that we laugh. My grandson was here for a few hours, and I asked him how old he thought I was. He said seventy-eight! I told him I was only sixty-one, and we just sat and laughed. We have to learn to not take life so seriously. It's good to laugh.

Today, laugh. Laugh at yourself. Find someone to laugh with. There are lots of serious things going on in the world, but we have to remember that everything is in Jesus's hands. And it's okay to laugh.

Have a blessed day!

March 9

As I sit and have my cup of coffee with Jesus, I was thinking about the things that we *hand over*. We talk about *handing over* our life to Jesus, and that is a good thing. However, sometimes, I think we *hand over* our minds to many other entities. We *hand over* our minds to our cell phones, to television, to social media. And we let other people tell us what we should be doing, what we should look like, even what we should be thinking!

How many times do you see people in a restaurant who, instead of enjoying a meal with others, are on their phones? Or people taking a walk or enjoying the beach; instead, they're on their phones. Most of the time, we don't even know we're doing this. We are handing over our lives! We do not let the world control our bodies, and we should not let it control our minds!

Today, I am going to think for myself and limit the time I look at my phone. I'm going to let the Lord speak to me instead of listening to the ramblings of the world. I'm going to *hand over* my mind to the Lord.

Have a great and free day!

March 10

As I sit and have my cup of coffee with Jesus, I was thinking about the word *restore*! In Acts 3:21, it says, "Jesus must remain in heaven until the time comes for God to *restore* everything, as He promised long ago through His holy prophets." Have you ever known someone who *restored* old cars or old furniture or anything else to make it new? I love watching shows on TV where they take a house that is falling apart and *restore* it.

God has chosen to *restore* us! He takes our sinful nature, our failings, our life situations, and He *restores* us. We become the ultimate restoration. Sometimes, we need to stop and look back at all that God has done in our lives, constantly *restoring* us. We are a piece of art in the works.

Today, take a moment to look back at where God has taken you, and see where you are today. Look at the trials and tribulations, and instead, see the *triumphs*! Isn't it great to know that we have a God that doesn't look at us for who we are, but rather sees our potential and *restores* us?

Have a beautiful day!

March 11

As I sit and have my cup of coffee with Jesus, I was thinking about *self-awareness*. The Bible tells us in 1 Timothy 4:16, "Keep a close watch on yourself and on the teaching. Persist in this, for by doing so you will save both yourself and your hearers." It is important for us to have self-awareness and self-reflection. It says in 2 Corinthians 13:5, "Examine yourselves, to see whether you are in the faith. Test yourselves. Or do you not realize this about yourselves, that Jesus Christ is in you?"

Every day, when we wake up and when we go to bed, we should do some self-reflection. We should reflect on and be aware of how our day has gone, of whether we responded like Christ, or in ways we can be better. True self-awareness helps us to see the Christ that lives in us.

Today, take time to reflect and be aware of self and the Christ that lives in you. When you do, you become a light in a world where there is a lot of darkness, and we need the light more than ever.

Have a blessed day being aware of the great *gift* you are!

March 12

As I sit and have my cup of coffee with Jesus, I was thinking about the word *freedom*. Epictetus said, "But anyone who can be restricted, coerced, or pushed into something against what they will is a slave." The Bible tells us in Galatians 5:1, "It is for *freedom* that Christ has set us free. Stand firm, then, and do not let yourselves be a burden again by a yoke of slavery." Psalm 119:45 says, "I will walk about in *freedom*, for I have sought out your precepts."

It is good for us to reflect on *freedom*, that we have choices, that our choices should be guided by God's Word. Oftentimes, we can feel controlled or our freedoms are taken away by others, but our *freedom* comes from Christ and our relationship with Him. It allows us to live and preach the Good News.

Today, embrace the *freedom* that Jesus called you to. Live in *freedom*, not controlled, coerced, or restricted, but in the true freedom of faith. It is liberating to live in Christ's *freedom*. The Good News of Jesus Christ lives through you!

Be free and have a blessed day!

March 13

As I sit and have my cup of coffee with Jesus, I was reflecting how much we *rush* and how much *noise* we create. So I came up with the phrase, "Not the *rush*, but the *hush*." It is important for our souls that we slow down and take moments of quiet. Sometimes, we fill our time with noise.

Psalm 46:10 says, "Be still and know that I am God." Psalm 62:5 says, "For God alone, oh my soul, wait in silence, for my hope is from Him." Sometimes, we need to quiet ourselves down so that we can hear His voice. That will take away the rush and busyness of the day and calm our hearts.

So today, on this beautiful morning, don't *rush*, but *hush*, and listen to the sound of His voice as He leads you through the day!

Have a blessed day.

March 14

As I sit and have my cup of coffee with Jesus, I was thinking of the word *change*. As much as we don't always like it, everything is *changing*. When we try to hold on to things too tightly, we struggle with *change*. Jesus teaches us to live in the moment, to allow change to happen because He has a plan for us.

The scriptures tell us in 2 Corinthians 5:17, "Therefore, if anyone is in Christ, the new creation has come: the old has gone. The new is here!" In Isaiah 43:19, it says, "See, I am doing a new thing! Now it springs up; do you not perceive it? I am making a way in the wilderness and streams in the wasteland."

Today, embrace change. Give praise to God for the changes that are happening in your life, in your family, in your community, and in our world. Don't be afraid of change; rather, know that it is a gift from God.

Have a blessed day embracing change!

March 15

As I sit and have my cup of coffee with Jesus, I was thinking about *self-trust*. It's hard sometimes to *trust* ourselves, but it is also the core of our existence. If we believe that Christ lives in us, then *trusting* ourselves is very important. Both doubt and fear are our enemies. Anxiety, confusion, or depression are against the very spirit of God that lives in us.

We learn *self-trust* by listening, by making mistakes, and then by *trusting* ourselves anyway. We learn *self-trust* by listening to God who lives within us. In reality, we know what is best for us, and we know what takes us down. We have to learn to *trust* ourselves! We can look for others to support and help us, but we have to *trust* ourselves. When we stand in our own *trust* and in our own light, Christ lives in us. First Philippians 4:13 says, "I can do all things through Him who strengthens me." Psalm 28:7 says, "The Lord is my strength and my shield; and in Him my heart *trusts*, and I am helped. My heart exults, and with my song I will give thanks to Him."

Today, listen to your inner voice; it is the Christ that lives within you who guides you. Trust in yourself and say the beautiful prayer of the Divine Mercy, "Jesus, I *trust* in you!"

Have a blessed day!

March 16

As I sit and have my cup of coffee with Jesus, I was thinking about the word *praise*. The dictionary says *praise* is the expression of approval or admiration for someone or something. Every morning, we need to wake up and *praise* God. We've been given the chance for a new day, a new beginning.

The scriptures remind us about *praise*. We need to praise God in the good times and the bad. David says in Psalm 68:19, "*Praise* be to the Lord, the God our Savior, who daily bears are burdens." To *praise* is to give thanks. Deuteronomy 7:9 says, "I *praise* you, God, for You keep your covenant of love to a thousand generations of those who love You and keep Your commandments."

Today, we *praise* God for the rain, we *praise* Him for life, and we even praise Him for the trials we endure! *Praise* is the highest form of prayer.

So today, *praise* the Lord and have a blessed day!

March 17

As I sit and have my cup of coffee with Jesus, I was thinking about the power of *positive thinking*. It is so easy to look around and complain and feel that everything is wrong. But as Christians, we are to see God's hand in everything. Maybe you've spent a lifetime around negative people and have absorbed the disease. Negative thinking empowers the problem.

We need to find balance in our lives and open our eyes to what is good each day. We need to bring the *positive* message of the gospel. Positive energy heals, brings love, and transforms! The scriptures remind us in Philippians 4:8, "Finally, brothers and sisters, whatever is true, whatever is honorable, whatever is just, whatever is pure, whatever is lovely, whatever is commendable, if there is any excellence, if there is anything worthy of praise, think about these things."

Today, make it a *positive* day. Fill the morning with positive thoughts. Today, bring the *positive* message of Christ to the world.

Have a blessed day!

March 18

As I sit and have my cup of coffee with Jesus, I was thinking about the word *generous*. Have you ever met anyone in your life that is, by nature, generous? People who sometimes share what they have, sometimes share good advice, or sometimes just share a listening ear are generous. Scriptures tell us in Proverbs 11:25, "A generous person will prosper; whoever refreshes others will be refreshed." And it says in 2 Corinthians 9:11, "You will be enriched in every way so that you can be *generous* on every occasion, and through us your generosity will result in thanksgiving to God." *Generosity*, then, becomes a prayer. Would people say that you are *generous* with your gifts?

Today is a good day to examine your own sense of generosity and compare it to God's generosity to you. If you are like me, you know you have a lot of work to do!

Have a blessed and *generous* day!

March 19

As I sit and have my cup of coffee with Jesus, I was thinking about *working out*. I seem to be very disciplined in my prayer life and I like routine, but working out takes a lot of effort for me. I know I should do it, I feel better once I've done it, and I know it's good for my body, so why do I struggle? And yet, as I sit and have my cup of coffee with Jesus, I'm thinking of all the ways to get out of my *workout* this morning. Pancakes sound so much better!

However, today, I am going to listen to my inner voice that tells me I need this in more ways than one. It will help me in the ministry God calls me to do today. It will help me to think more clearly and to feel good. I am going to make it part of my prayer today to exercise.

So today, join me. Get out and take care of your body. Take a walk, go on a hike, go to the gym, do something to continue to celebrate health and God's call to take care of the temple of the Holy Spirit.

I'm heading into the gym right now, but maybe I'll go for pancakes after my workout!

Have a blessed day!

March 20

As I sit and have my cup of coffee with Jesus, I was thinking about the word *promise*. Have you ever made a *promise* to God and then not kept it? I think, over the course of my life, there were many times I tried to bargain or make promises to God. Even carrying out my Lenten *promises* are hard! The powerful thing is that, though I may fail in keeping my *promises* to the Lord, He never fails to keep His promises to me.

Jesus's *promises* are real. He doesn't promise us fame, wealth, or riches, but He does *promise* us joy, peace, and understanding. John 15:9 says, "As the Father has loved Me, so I have loved you. Now remain in My love." His promise to love us and to be our light is His gift. Studying and reading the scriptures helps us to remain in His love and to embrace His promises. He is faithful!

Today, I am going to reflect on His *promises* and remember that the closer I stay to Him, the better I can live out my promise to serve Him. Isn't it great to know we have someone in our lives who keeps their promises?

Have a great day.

March 21

As I sit and have my cup of coffee with Jesus, I was thinking about a phrase I read in a reflection, "Cross Bearers for Christ." What a powerful phrase, as each of us are called to be *cross bearers*! Being a *cross bearer*, like Simon of Cyrene, means to take action, to not be afraid to get into the arena, to use our brokenness for service. Many people sat back and watched Jesus go by, but Simon of Cyrene took action.

We hear in scripture, Matthew 16:24–26, "If anyone wishes to come after Me, He must deny himself, and take up his cross and follow Me." The world will always remember the name of Simon of Cyrene because he helped Jesus with the cross. We all have *crosses to bear*, and we need each other to help to carry them.

Today, think of friends who need help carrying the cross and become a *cross bearer*. Call them, visit them, enter into their passion, and be a friend. What a beautiful world it would be if we helped each other carry our crosses.

Have a blessed day!

March 22

As I sit and have my cup of coffee with Jesus, I was thinking about *retreat*. Oftentimes, I think that I need to go to another country, or to the mountains, or to the ocean to take a *retreat*, to get away from things, to find that peaceful balance, and to rest. But the best place to make a *retreat* is within our own souls! We don't really need to go anywhere to bring ourselves into the peace of God. Psalm 46:10 says, "Be still and know that I am God!" And Psalm 23:1–2 says, "The Lord is my shepherd; I shall not want. He makes me to lie down in green pastures. He leads me beside still waters. He restores my soul."

Every day, we need to do a mini-retreat. We need to stop, close our eyes, breathe, and be in the moment. This calms the mind, gets rid of anxiety, and bring us back into our souls.

Today, I'm going to take five mini-*retreats* between appointments, errands, and unplanned events. I am going to stop and be still and know that I am with God.

Have a blessed day!

March 23

As I sit and have my cup of coffee with Jesus, I was thinking about *perseverance* in *prayer*. I was doing a little study on Elijah when I discovered what a powerful prayer he made. It was bold and full of confidence. Elijah did not beat around the bush or even bargain with God. He believed God's promises, and he prayed with authority.

In studying Elijah (1 Kings 18:20–40), we learn that we do not need to pray in secret; we need to be bold and strong when we pray. God tells us to come boldly into His presence. That is very powerful, because we are followers of Jesus Christ, and we can believe and trust in His promises.

Today, I am going to pray *boldly* to my God. I am going to trust His promises to me and pray with confidence for all the people and situations in which I need His guidance. So whatever you are praying about, pray with *perseverance* and *confidence,* and trust that God hears you and will keep His promises.

Have a blessed day!

March 24

As I sit and have my cup of coffee with Jesus, I was thinking about the *news*. I used to faithfully watch the *news*, but over the past few years, I find I don't watch it much anymore. It is always all *bad news*. I really don't know who to believe or if they are even reporting the truth. That is why I have substituted my time watching the *news* with reading the Good News.

If you want to find peace and balance in your life, it's necessary to get to know Christ. One of the best ways to do that is to read His Word, the Good News. The scriptures are better at helping us through our problems than anything else.

So today, instead of turning on the television or reading the newspaper, pick up your Bible and read the Good News. I'll give you a hint: it's about love, joy, forgiveness, and peace! That should whet your appetite.

Have a blessed day!

March 25

As I sit and have my cup of coffee with Jesus, I was thinking of a quote by Samuel Rutherford. He says, "The secret formula of the saints is: When I am in the cellar of *affliction*, I look for the Lord's choicest wines." This quote caught my eye on many levels. First, I like wine, and not only have I had personal experience being in the cellar of affliction, I have been blessed over the years with people sharing their stories with me of their own afflictions.

Whether it be the loss of a loved one, a struggle with addiction, or fear of living in anxiety or depression, one time or another, we all know what it's like to have entered into the cellar of the *affliction*. The key is to taste the choicest wines. In our pain, we must hold on to the only thing that leads us through our affliction, the blood of Christ! We become one with the passion of our Lord. He drank from the cup and passed it on to us. There is nothing for us to fear!

Today, look at how Jesus has carried you through afflictions in your life. He has never abandoned you or left you alone. He invites you to drink from the cup! Hold it with two hands and taste the choicest wine!

Have a blessed day!

March 26

As I sit and have my cup of coffee with Jesus, I was thinking about *grief*. I spoke with a number of people in the last few weeks who've experienced the loss of loved ones. When we are in the midst of that pain, we experience *grief*. One of my friends shared with me a quote that says, "And when nobody wakes you up in the morning, and when nobody waits for you at night, and when you can do whatever you want...what do you call it, freedom or loneliness?"

That is a lot to think about. Whenever there is loss, there is great change. I think when we are in grief, our emotions go back and forth. Every situation is a little different, but the effects of *grief* are profound! Another quote says, "*Grief* is just love with nowhere to go!"

If you or someone you know is experiencing grief, turn to our Lord! Let Him embrace you and your uncertainty! Jesus says, "Come to Me, all you who are weary, and I will give you rest."

Today, reach out to a friend who may be grieving, or if you yourself are grieving, spend some time with the Lord and feel His comforting embrace.

Have a blessed day!

March 27

As I sit and have my cup of coffee with Jesus, I was thinking about the word *consistency*. I think it is important that we have consistency in our lives. Consistency in the way in which we live, in our prayer lives, and especially in our relationships with the Lord!

Consistency means acting or doing something in the same way over time. Scriptures tell us, "Jesus Christ is the same yesterday and today and forever" (Hebrews 13:8). I feel I am consistent with my prayer life...I wish sometimes I were as consistent with my workouts and my diet!

Today, I am going to strive to be more consistent in my walk with the Lord, taking time for real prayer, for silence, and for listening to the direction of His Spirit.

Have a blessed day!

March 28

As I sit and have my cup of coffee with Jesus, I was thinking about Palm Sunday. On Palm Sunday, the passion of Christ is read, and we transition into Holy Week. We are entering into a special time. The passion of Christ is the basis of our faith.

When you go to church on Palm Sunday, you will receive a palm that has been blessed. It is a symbol of the journey that we've been on, and it has a very profound meaning. Many people have entered into the passion of Christ in a unique way, with loved ones who have been sick or who have even passed away. We have to *trust* that Christ is leading us to a greater awareness of His love as He did in His passion.

Today, take time to pray for the sick, reflect on the past year, and see what lessons you have learned about *love*. I highly recommend watching the Passion of Christ. I watch it every year to remind me of the sacrifice that was made for me.

Have a blessed day and a beautiful journey into this *holy time*!

March 29

As I sit and have my cup of coffee with Jesus, I was thinking of the word *neighbor*. I am blessed to live in a wonderful neighborhood. I don't think a day goes by that I don't see someone doing something kind for someone else. Yesterday, as I sat on my porch on a beautiful day, I saw a neighbor across the street take some food to another neighbor who has been under the weather. I watched other families ride by on their bikes and stop to say hello. And there were lots of dog walkers and people out planting flowers in their gardens, all taking time to stop and chat.

We even have a *neighbor* who, every morning, goes all through the neighborhood, checking on people, bringing cards by for people to sign for special occasions. I have even been blessed with some of her baked goods and bouquets of sweet peas. It's important to get to know your *neighbors*. So much fear has come into our world that people are afraid to get to know one another.

Today, I am going to pray for my *neighborhood* and see what I can do to be a better *neighbor*. Neighborhoods are small communities, and together, we can do great things. So today, be a great *neigh-*

bor. Get to know the people around you and try to build a community based on peace and love. Jesus would expect nothing less.

Have a blessed day!

March 30

As I sit and have my cup of coffee with Jesus, I was thinking about the word *forgiveness*. I was reflecting on all that Jesus went through. I think of all the people He had to forgive on His journey, the disciples who abandoned Him, the people who mocked Him, and of course, those who led to His crucifixion. And then I think about all the people I need to forgive on my journey. I think of the people in my life who have hurt me or betrayed me. Sometimes, it's easier for me to plan their demise than to forgive them!

But I know what Jesus expects of me, to forgive seventy times seven. In Ephesians 4:32, the scriptures say, "Be kind and compassionate to one another, forgiving each other, just as Christ God forgave you." And Matthew 6:14 says, "For if you forgive other people when they sin against you, your Heavenly Father will also forgive you."

Today, I'm going to name the people that I need to forgive and pray that God opens my heart to that gift. We have the gift of a God that never stops forgiving us, and He calls us to do the same.

Have a blessed day!

March 31

As I sit and have my cup of coffee with Jesus, I was thinking about the word *anticipation*. Think about all the times you got really excited about something and the anticipation that builds up. The Easter season has always been that for me. The processions and the washing of the feet on Holy Thursday, the solemnity and adoration of the cross on Good Friday, and all of the baptisms and sacraments during the Easter season have filled me with joy.

With all of the changes that have taken place in my life, I'm working hard to be excited about all of these moments because this is the highlight of our Christian faith. It's really how you look at things. I am excited to celebrate the Risen Lord. Like most people, I'm ready to roll back the stone and come out of the tomb!

So these next few days, with the heart of gratitude, I'm going to celebrate the journey of faith, a journey through good times and bad, sickness and health, a time that Jesus reminds us He is in charge! I am in *anticipation* of miracles!

Have a blessed day, and remember to watch for miracles!

April 1

As I sit and have my cup of coffee with Jesus, I was thinking about the Easter Triduum, which falls on a different day every year. These holy days begin with Holy Thursday. The liturgy celebrated at church has the traditional washing of the feet, the celebration of the Eucharist, and a procession of the Eucharist to a special place for adoration, all preparing for Good Friday.

I have always loved the Holy Thursday liturgy. It reminds us of our call to *service* and of the great gift that Christ gave us in the Eucharist. During Holy Thursday, I like to reflect on the ways in which I have been of service to others and my community this past year. I like to reflect on the gift of the Eucharist and how it continues to be the center of my life.

So today, I repeat the words, *slow down, simplify* and *sanctify* this day. Take time to reflect on Jesus's call to service and the gift He gave us in the breaking of the bread. It's time to get ready to *greet* the Risen Lord. It's time to get ready to enter into His passion!

Have a Holy Easter season!

April 2

As I sit and have my cup of coffee with Jesus, I was thinking about Good Friday. I've always wondered why they called it Good Friday. It never seemed that good to me. Last night, I watched *The Passion of the Christ* by Mel Gibson. I have seen the movie many times, but I get something new out of it every time I watch it. This time, I was focused on other characters, on Peter, on His mother, Mary, on Simon of Cyrene, and on Veronica. Each of them had their own struggles in life and yet intimately entered into the passion of Christ.

We, too, are called to enter into His passion, to die to self, to be honest with ourselves, and to ask who do we truly serve. Peter denied Christ, yet later embraced His cross. Simon stepped forward to remind us that we are not alone. Veronica was brave and pushed through the soldiers to wipe the face of Christ. And Mary had the courage to witness her Son's suffering and still trust the Father that this was all part of a greater plan.

Throughout this holy season, reflect on the *cross*. Through the passion, we are set *free*, free from the bondage of sin, free from the slavery of ego. We were invited into a wonderful life centered on the cross. Without Good Friday, we would never know this freedom.

Have a blessed and reflective day!

April 3

As I sit and have my cup of coffee with Jesus, I was reflecting on the *tomb*. From Good Friday until Easter Sunday, Jesus laid in the *tomb*. How many times in our lives have we stayed in the *tomb*, the *tomb* of despair and depression, the tomb of grief or fear? Often, we have experienced disconnection and isolation that is the *tomb*.

As we go journey through this holy season, the special time in the church when people are welcomed in, are baptized, and receive the sacraments, it is a powerful reminder that we need to come out of the *tomb*. We have to trust in the power of the Risen Lord and open our hearts for change, renewal, and joy in life. We have to come out of the *tomb*!

Today, present to the Lord your worries and fears, let go of any anger and resentment you hold on to, and be prepared for a new year. Live in the *presence* of the Risen Lord!

Roll back the stone, and come on out!

April 4

Today, as I sit with my cup of coffee with Jesus, I was thinking about Easter! There is not much more to say than He has risen! And now it's time for us to *rise* out of the darkness and to celebrate the victory He made for us over death.

This Easter season, celebrate with your family, count your blessings, and know that this is going to be an amazing year. Celebrate all the painful lessons you learned this past year and ask our Lord to bring you into His light.

May God bless you and your family this Easter season, and may you experience the freedom, peace, and love of the Risen Lord!

Have a blessed day.

April 5

As I sit and have my cup of coffee with Jesus, I continue to allow myself to experience all aspects of the Easter season. The Easter message is that Jesus has *risen*. Every day I try to experience the presence of the Risen Lord in the beauty of His creation. As spring is upon us and everything is coming to life, we, too, should be coming to life. The Word of God becomes alive!

During the Easter season, we need to keep alive the Spirit of the living God. We need to take the joy that we are loved by One who gave His very life so that we might live in His joy.

Today, begin your day with gratitude and a smile on your face, knowing that you are loved! With each day, the light of Christ will guide us out of the darkness of the world. It's happening now; just look around and give glory to God!

Have a blessed day!

April 6

As I sit and have my cup of coffee with Jesus, I was thinking about *anger*. In the last few days, a number of people have shared with me the anger they have. They have either been hurt by someone or are frustrated with what is happening in their lives, and some don't even know what they are angry about. I have learned over the years that *anger* only destroys the person who holds on to it.

We need to look at our lives and be truthful about what we're angry about, and most of the time, it's about our own choices. Isn't it wonderful that we have a God that does not hold grudges or remain angry, but continually challenges us to be more focused on Him than holding on to anger? Sometimes, it is easier said than done.

The scriptures tell us in James 1:19–20, "Know this, my beloved brothers: let every person be quick to hear, slow to speak, slow to anger; for the anger of man does not produce the righteousness of God."

Today, if you're angry at someone or some situation or even yourself, ask God to help you let it go and focus on His love and mercy and watch the anger dissipate.

Have a blessed day!

April 7

Today, as I sit and have my cup of coffee with Jesus, I continue my reflection on *anger*. Anger is a real emotion, and we should not deny it. Rather, we have to be very careful and observe it. I have read some great quotes about anger. One said, "Anger doesn't solve anything, it builds nothing, but it can destroy everything." Another one says, "Speak when you are angry, and you'll make the best speech you'll never forget!"

Even Jesus got angry. You remember the story of Jesus in the temple; He turned over the tables. We cannot ignore anger, but we certainly need to be careful when we allow it to control us. Aristotle said, "Anyone can become angry—that is easy, but to be angry with the right person, and to the right degree, and at the right time, and for the right purpose, and in the right way—that is not within everybody's power and is not easy."

When we take our *anger* to prayer, God can help us soften the blow, help us to regroup, and breathe his grace into the moment. Ralph Waldo Emerson said, "For every minute you remain angry, you give up sixty seconds of peace of mind." Today, lift up your *anger* and learn to calm yourself, give space and time to whoever or whatever angers you, and allow God in! Don't waste another minute!

Have a blessed day.

April 8

As I sit and have my cup of coffee with Jesus, I was reflecting on *inner stillness*. A few years ago, I went through a personal crisis. Even thinking about it brings tension to my body. During that time, I was filled with intense anxiety and helplessness. I was overwhelmed by circumstances. I felt paralyzed. During that time, inside my heart, I could hear only a whisper, "Be still, and know that I am God." Something greater than me and my circumstances were holding me together.

This is the Easter experience, finding that stillness, that moment where we can find the truth that God is *with* us. Don't get me wrong, it was a long journey, but the voice got louder, and I became still. The only thing I could embrace were those words, "Be still, and know that I am God."

Today, as I begin my day, I take a moment to be *still* and listen to that voice that speaks from my inner soul, "Be still and know that I am God," and I know that will bring me to the peace that only comes from Him!

Find that stillness, and you will find His *peace*!

April 9

As I sit and have my cup of coffee with Jesus, I was reflecting on 2 Corinthians 12:10. One of the translations says, "Therefore, I take pleasure in being without strength, being insulted, experiencing emergencies, and being chased and forced into a corner for Christ's sake; for when I am without strength, I am *dynamic*." So many people I speak with are going through difficult times, yet they are amazing, *dynamic* people.

When I hear stories of what people endure and yet claim Christ for their strength, I am inspired. They may be sorting through things or trying to make sense of the pain they carry, but what I really see is their witness to the love of God in them. These are true heroes of faith.

Today, I am going to pray specifically for those who are going through difficult times, that they may continue to be witnesses of faith. These are the people who are *dynamic* and inspirational, not because everything is easy for them, but because Christ lives through them and their suffering!

Have a blessed day. Thank you for your witness. You know who you are…you inspire me!

April 10

As I sit and have my cup of coffee with Jesus, I was thinking about the gift of *time*. Sometimes, *time* goes very fast, and sometimes, it seems to just stand still. Sometimes, I find myself wasting *time*, and then there are other times when I feel like I have no *time* at all. When we put our lives in the hands of God, we can find *time* for everything He wants us to experience.

When we don't put off our *time* to pray, make *time* to get enough sleep, when we make *time* to exercise, we will begin to find the balance of *time*. When we find the balance, we have *time* for everything. We have *time* for family, for work, for service, and most of all, for our Lord.

The scriptures tell us there is a *time* for everything. So today, ask the Lord how He wants you to spend the *time* that he has given you on this day. He always gives us enough *time* for us to open ourselves to Him.

Have a blessed day! He has provided just enough *time* for you to do everything He needs you to do!

April 11

As I sit and have my cup of coffee with Jesus, I was thinking about a book I read years ago, entitled *Don't Sweat the Small Stuff*. I know this is true, but it is harder to practice living it. It makes me wonder why I make such a long to-do list every day, why I have trouble sitting still and reflecting, and how I get annoyed when something I plan doesn't go just the way I wanted.

When we choose to follow Jesus, we can't sweat the small stuff. Jesus is always bringing us sacred interruptions to see if we can find the *holiness* in the moment. We can learn that we do not have to control the moment, but that we can actually be present in it.

Whether it be a house that needs to be cleaned or a flat tire or endless lists, our attitude makes all the difference. Are we serving our to-do list or our Lord's? Can we see the lessons in the sacred interruptions? Are we holding on to the past or embracing the present? When we strive to put Jesus in the center of our lives, it is all small stuff!

Today, I will strive to see Jesus in all the simple tasks, the small things, and make them prayers of *gratitude*.

I think I will put that on my list!

April 12

As I sit and have my cup of coffee with Jesus, I was reflecting on Divine Mercy! In the dictionary, *divine* is defined as "of, or from God" and *mercy* is defined as "compassion or forgiveness shown towards someone whom it is within one's power to punish or harm." What a powerful gift Divine Mercy is!

When someone wrongs me or hurts me or someone I love, my mind automatically goes to revenge. I can plot their downfall, but I know Jesus asks much more of me. He reminds me of the *mercy* that He has shown me in those times when I did not live up to being the best person I can be. It's an endless *mercy*, loving us for who we are, loving us and our sinfulness, and never giving up on us. He only asked that we do the same in return.

We've all been hurt, attacked, abandoned, or deeply wounded, but Jesus calls us to share His *mercy*. So today, let us think of those we need to forgive and lift them up to Jesus. Let us ask Jesus for the strength to be merciful to them as He has been merciful to us.

Have a blessed day!

April 13

As I sit and have my cup of coffee with Jesus, I was thinking about a phrase I came across yesterday, "*stand firm*." I found it in 1 Corinthians 16:13, "Be watchful, *stand firm* in faith, be strong." And

Ephesians 6:11 says, "Put on the whole armor of God that you may be able to *stand firm* against the schemes of the devil." In 1 Peter 5, it says, "Resist him, *stand firm* in your faith, knowing that the same kinds of suffering are being experienced by others throughout the world."

Sometimes, it's easy to want to throw in the towel or to give up the fight. Sometimes, we begin to lose our patience or become negative and critical. We can gain strength from the words of Christ, "*Stand firm.*" Stand firm that this, too, will pass. *Stand firm* that we can make a difference. *Stand firm* that we can grow and become better people. *Stand firm* in the Word and presence of Jesus, even in the storm.

Today, let us *stand firm* in our belief that all is in the hands of Jesus. Jesus walks with us through our trials; they will bring us to a deeper relationship with Him.

Stand firm and smile!

April 14

As I sit and have my cup of coffee with Jesus, I was reflecting on Matthew 28:20, "I am with you always." Those are amazing and powerful words, especially if you're going through a difficult time. Maybe you're going through a difficulty in your relationship, with finances, health, or just full of anxiety…that is when you need to reflect on these words.

It is powerful to realize that we are never alone, to know that we are always loved, to know that we are always forgiven. This is the powerful promise that our Lord makes to us. So if you're frustrated, hurt, angry, or worried, reflect on the words of Jesus who says, "I am with you always," and know that you are in good hands.

Today is a new day, and Jesus wants to walk with you and all you need to do is invite Him in.

Have a blessed day. I know that He is there with you!

April 15

As I sit and have my cup of coffee with Jesus, I was thinking about this *new* day. There are some things I need to get done today. I have a number of appointments and people I need to check on, but I really want to be *present and positive*. I want to be *present* in my attitude, in my speech, and in my awareness throughout the day. I want to acknowledge all of God's blessings as they take place.

It is easy to become overwhelmed with what we have planned for the day, but it is even more amazing when we change your *attitude* and awaken. As the sun rises this morning, I see God's creation coming alive. Today, I'm going to work on my attitude, praising God while I'm unloading the dishwasher, while meeting with friends, and while reading and writing.

Today, pour yourself a cup of coffee and take a few moments to make this the best day. For this is the day the Lord has made, let us rejoice and be glad in it.

I am listening to Louis Armstrong singing "What a Wonderful World." Google it! https://www.youtube.com/watch?v=VqhCQZaH4Vs

April 16

As I sit and have my cup of coffee with Jesus, I was reflecting on the phrase, "God alone suffices." What wisdom we can gain from the saints! As the sun is rising, I look out and see a beautiful day on the horizon, so what do we have to fear? Sometimes, we have to try to remove the negativity in our thinking and just bask in the presence of the Almighty.

Today reminds me of when I was a child. We would ride our bikes in the neighborhood as long as we were home before the streetlights came on. We might go to the park or swim at someone's house; there was always time to enjoy the day and each other. Today, everybody is busy, everyone is in a hurry. I would love to remind you what "busy" stands for:

B: Being
U: Under
S: Satan's
Y: Yoke

So today, don't get too busy. Make time for people, put a smile on your face, and have a wonderful day!

April 17

As I sit and have my cup of coffee with Jesus, I was thinking about how God *trains* us. Last night, I saw a father on his bike. He was followed by his five-year-old son on his bike with training wheels. I thought that is how the Father leads us, He gives us training "wills!" He teaches us gradually how to surrender our will to His.

We spend so much of our time working for titles, a bigger house, more money, and our egos can grow very strong. We lose our focus and purpose, and God steps in to teach us to surrender. We do not have to be afraid, because He is always with us, training us, reminding us, and picking us up and loving us. We all need training!

Today, think about what God is training you for! Are you listening, are you following, are you surrendering? That boy, on his bike with training wheels, held on tight but never took his eyes off the Father.

Have a blessed day!

April 18

As I sit and have my cup of coffee with Jesus, I was thinking about the power of *listening*. Being able to *listen* to others, to creation, and especially to God takes effort. It is easy to talk, to try to make your point, and for some, it's easy to argue, but to really take time to listen to what someone has to say is an art.

Have you ever sat outside and listened to the birds sing, or the crashing of the ocean waves, or even to majestic silence? When we *listen*, we slow our brains down and take away the noise of the world. It is easy to pray by rambling off words or repeating prayers, but the gift of prayer is *listening* to the voice of God speaking to our hearts!

Today, on this beautiful morning, as the sun prepares to come up, I am going to say the prayers and read the reflections that I do every day, but today, I am going to make a special effort to *listen* to God tell me of the *glorious* things He has planned for me today. I am sure that His list of things for me to do is far greater and life-giving than the one that I have prepared!

Have a blessed day and *listen*!

April 19

As I sit and have my cup of coffee with Jesus, I was thinking about my mother. My mother died during the Easter season. My father had passed away only seven months before her. It was during the Easter Vigil that I was given a note telling me that my mom had passed. I was blessed to have my parents live with me during the last two years of their lives; I learned a lot from both of them.

So today is about remembering, and though there is a sadness, I can't help but be filled with joy of a life well-lived. My mother spoke her mind, she challenged me, and she loved me! I think it's good for all of us to remember and celebrate. So today is going to be a wonderful day, remembering my mother who had a tremendous impact on my life.

If you still have your mother, reach out to her today and let her know how much you love her. If your mother has passed away, remind her of your love. If your mother was not there for you, forgive her.

Have a blessed day…remembering.

April 20

As I sit and have my cup of coffee with Jesus, I was thinking about the word *connection*. In some ways, I believe all of life is about connections, connecting with God, connecting with others, and connecting with our true selves. Today, I woke up so early, I put toast in the toaster, and nothing happened. I forgot to plug it in! See, it's all about connections.

Throughout our lives, we have connections that are severed—death! We have connections that are fragile, connections that are short-lived, and lifetime connections too. It is all about the connections. Take some time today and think about the connections you cherish. Maybe your marriage needs to be plugged back in. Maybe you need to reconnect with your child, an old friend, or most importantly, God.

The best thing about connecting with God is that He never disconnects from us. We just have to take a moment and focus on the reality that He always stays plugged into us and claim it.

Today, it's about *connections* and celebrating the gift that God gives us connecting *our* souls.

Have a blessed day!

April 21

As I sit and have my cup of coffee with Jesus with my new mug, I was thinking about the need to *reach out*. Sometimes in our daily walk, our energy is low. We might be fighting depression, or we just feel overwhelmed with problems, and that's when we should hear the words from our Lord, *reach out*!

In times like this, we need to go outside of ourselves and reach out. Call a friend, visit someone who is sick, write a card to somebody who is in a hospital, make sandwiches for the homeless, do something to get out of self—*reach out*!

And while you are reaching out, *reach out* to the Lord. Ask Him to bring light into your life and into your heart. Ask Him to inspire you so you can inspire others, and ask Him to lift you out of darkness into his loving embrace.

Reach out!

April 22

As I sit and have my cup of coffee with Jesus, I was thinking about how important it is to have a positive attitude in *prayer*. Sometimes, *prayer* can be rather routine, like marking something off the to-do list. Sometimes, *prayer* is deep and contemplative. What I have come to realize is that my attitude is very important. I am bringing myself present to the Lord and allowing my *soul* to reach out to touch *my* Creator.

When I have a *positive* attitude, my *prayer* is a powerful prayer. I find myself full of gratitude and blessings. The problems have not gone away and there's still a long list of things to do, but for that moment, I allow my soul to touch Him. With open arms, He embraces me and lets me know that everything is going to be *okay*, actually not just *okay*, but *wonderful*.

Today, take a moment to *pray*! *Pray* with thanksgiving and praise, *pray* with confidence and trust. Let me know what happens, because there's nothing like hearing someone share their story of meeting God face-to-face.

Have a blessed day!

April 23

As I sit and have my cup of coffee with Jesus, I was thinking about the word *balance*. It's not always easy to keep our spiritual, emotional, psychological, and physical life in *balance*. During my workout, my trainer always talks about *balance*, especially the older we get. She has us do all kinds of exercises to help us keep balanced.

I think the most difficult area for me to stay balanced is physically. If my workout partners did not come, I would probably be out getting a doughnut somewhere! But because they are diligent, my workout partners help me to find that balance. It is important to find people who can keep you accountable, especially in areas in which you find it most difficult to stay balanced.

Jesus wants us to live a *balanced* life! Thank you, workout partners, for keeping me balanced. I think I've kept this routine up for about fifteen years now. Even though I'm not excited when I see my trainer show up (I want a doughnut), I know it keeps me balanced.

Today, find someone to take a walk with, to go for a run with, to ride a bike with, and to find that physical *balance*.

Have a great day.

April 24

As I sit and have my cup of coffee with Jesus, I was thinking about the word *energy*. From the time my eyes open in the morning to the end of the day, my *energy* level changes. Have you ever met someone who drains you of your energy because of all their drama?

On the same note, have you ever met someone whose energy is so contagious that they lift your spirit?

As Christians, our *energy* (Spirit) needs to flow from our relationship with Christ. This is what made the disciples so dynamic. The Spirit of Christ was the *energy* that flowed out of them. How was your energy today? Are you tired, overwhelmed, angry, or sad? Then it's time to reconnect with our Lord and allow His *energy* to lift you up.

Today, be energized by the One who created you and loves you. And then take that *energy* and Spirit and spread it to our world. There is only one kind of real *energy*, and that is *energy* that comes from the Father, through the Son, in the Holy Spirit.

Have a blessed day!

April 25

As I sit and have my cup of coffee with Jesus, I was thinking about the expression "to gaze." It's another beautiful morning. The other day, I attended a wedding. I loved watching how the bride and groom gazed at each other. To gaze is to go out of self. Joni Eareckson Tada said, "I want to stay in the habit of 'glancing' at my problems and 'gazing' at the Lord." That is something that I want to do, too.

What a wonderful day it can be when we gaze upon the Lord and all of His wonderment, instead of being distracted by drama, violence, and fear.

Today, on this beautiful morning, *gaze* on the Lord with joy, amazement, and gratitude! It is a beautiful day when you *gaze* upon the love of the Father, Jesus Christ.

Have a wonderful day!

April 26

As I sit and have my cup of coffee with Jesus, I was thinking about the word *patience*. Philippians 4:6 says, "Do not be anxious about anything but in every situation, by prayer and petition, with thanksgiving, present your requests to God."

Some days, I find myself impatient with many things. I might be impatient with my children or my grandchildren, or with people who come to see me, or with the dog, or with my calendar; the list goes on and on. I'm trying to practice the art of pausing before I act or respond. During this pause, I take a breath and try to be conscious of what is actually going on.

So today, I am going to practice the art of being *patient*, not only with others, but also with myself. I am going to try to be mindful of the pause that I need to stay present in the moment so I can respond with love and care. Today, let's practice the art of being *patient* and celebrate our Lord, who is very *patient* with us.

Have a wonderful day!

April 27

As I sit and have my cup of coffee with Jesus, I was thinking about the need to *resist negativity*. Do you notice sometimes how some people carry a deep spirit of negativity with them? The negativity might be pent-up anger, a lack of forgiveness, or painful emotions. It's easy to be pulled into that negativity.

Sometimes, even as we try to be *positive*, that negative energy force throws us off balance. We have to be careful not to be pulled into the darkness. It does no one any good. To help someone come to the *light*, we do *not* have to step into their darkness. Be the *light*. Allow the light of Christ to shine through you.

Today, I'm going to be aware of the negativity that lies deep in the lives of people I love, and instead of trying to fix them, I'm going to be the *light*. I am going to allow the *light* of Christ to shine through me.

Have a blessed day!

April 28

As I sit and have my cup of coffee with Jesus, I was reflecting on the natural *rhythm* of life. Yesterday, I spent some hours just listening to the waves break, and I began to hear the rhythm. Whether it be the rhythm of our heartbeat or the rhythm of music, it has a calming effect.

In my own life, when I follow the natural *rhythm* of the universe, I find myself more energetic, more focused, and more at peace. When I go against the *rhythm* (which I also call spirit), I find myself swimming upstream, with never enough time, always in a hurry.

Today, I am going to try and stay in His rhythm. I am going to try to not let the distractions of the day take away the peace, the joy, and the love that flows from Him. It's great when we are in sync with God's Spirit.

Have a blessed day!

April 29

As I sit and have my cup of coffee with Jesus, I was reflecting on the word *harmony*. I even love the way it sounds, and I am blessed to have a daughter-in-law I love named Harmony, too!

When I live in *harmony* with the Lord, with my family, and with creation, then the love of God flows through me. When I live in the state of worry, fear, or dizziness, I tend to block that flow of God's love.

Each new day gives us an opportunity to live in *harmony*. We can choose whether we are going to have a bad hair day where everything is going to go wrong, or we can choose to bring joy and peace and love into the world.

Today, try bringing *harmony* into your life by allowing His divine mercy to flow through you. Romans 12:16 says, "Live in *harmony* with one another."

Have a harmonious day.

April 30

This morning, as I sit watching the sun come up, having my cup of coffee with Jesus, I was thinking about how Jesus is the Great Restorer.

I saw a documentary the other night where artists were restoring great works of art. Many works were torn or faded, and in some you couldn't really tell what the original even looked like. It reminded me of how it is in our lives. Sometimes, we feel torn or hurt, sometimes, we feel faded, and sometimes, we just lose ourselves completely. But we have nothing to fear, because Jesus does a redemptive work. He is a Salvage Artist.

If we allow Him, He can restore us, and not only restore us, *but* make us *new* again, with vibrant colors. He can restore us as a child of God. It says in Genesis 1:31, "And God saw everything that He had made, and behold, it was *very good.*"

Today, let the Master Artist restore and renew you! We are all a work of art.

Have a blessed day!

May 1

Watching the sunrise, having coffee with Jesus, it's another beautiful day! As Joni Eareckson Taday said, "I want to stay in the habit of 'glancing' at my problems and 'gazing' at the Lord."

God has work for us to do for the building of His kingdom. In the church, we celebrate the Feast of Saint Joseph, the worker. He is a shining example for all workers. Today, maybe we could spend less time focusing on our problems and spend more time in gratitude for all those who are able to work. Let us pray for the farmers, the factory workers, those in the medical profession, those in law enforcement, the emergency first responders, those who prepare food, the clerks, the teachers, and our government leaders. But let us also pray that today we do God's work as well. We must continue to build His kingdom.

Today, let us gaze on the Lord with joy, amazement, and gratitude. It is another beautiful day!

Saint Joseph, pray for us!

May 2

As I sit and have my cup of coffee with Jesus, I was thinking about the word *patience*. Philippians 4:6 says, "Do not be anxious about anything but in every situation, by prayer and petition, with thanksgiving, present your requests to God."

This past week, I found myself being impatient with my grandchildren and their homework, impatient with projects not getting accomplished, and with dishes in the sink. I really planned on blaming it on someone or something else, but I know I have always struggled with patience. Most of all, I noticed how impatient I am with myself.

Today, I am going to focus on being more patient, not being so anxious about things, but allow the Lord to bring each moment, each person, each experience to me and for me to embrace. I am going to strive today not to be petty, not to rush, but to be present.

And just as I was getting ready to offer up my prayers, my mind jumped to what I would do next after prayer! Do I have any waffles left? Where is my to-do list? But I caught myself and came back to being one with Him.

That is what the first five minutes of prayer is like for me. It looks like this may be a long day learning to be patient. Darn! I wanted it right now.

Have a patient, grace-filled day.

May 3

Today, enjoying my coffee with Jesus, I am reminded that joy and happiness are two different things. Happiness is good, but it is temporary. Joy is that deep connection with our Lord that brings peace, even when everything is not going well. Joy brings peaceful assurance of God's presence. My awareness of joy and the blessings that God brings can make a regular day a day full of blessings.

I experienced a deep joy yesterday when I watched a newborn baby and his family walk over to their grandparents' house on our block. A week before, the child was still inside his mother, and today, he is here, and the family was so full of joy. The gift of receiving joy, which comes from God, is that we have to share it. Then it becomes contagious.

Today, experience the joy that only God can bring. And then share it, share it with your spouse, share it with your children, share it with someone who may need to hear from you today. For this is the day the Lord has made (and it is full of joy), let us rejoice and be glad in it.

And don't forget to share it!

May 4

Today is another absolutely beautiful morning, having coffee with Jesus. Each day, I reflect on the daily readings, followed by a devotional, the office, and the rosary. At the end of Mass, I was thinking of how easy it is to know a lot about God but not to know Him.

Don't get me wrong. All of that reading and prayer is not a waste of time but should lead to a deeper desire to spend time with Him, to wait quietly and patiently to hear His voice. It should lead to an increased desire to talk to Him, to speak from the heart, to slow down enough to share with Him the yearnings of the heart. It should be a time to dedicate this new day to Him and a desire to be open to the plans He has for you, to see Him throughout your day.

Today, add to your time with Him in *silence*. Clear your mind, breathe deeply, and be in His presence. How can it not be the best day ever when He is present to us and we recognize it?

Have a Christ-filled day!

May 5

As I am watching the sunrise, having my cup of coffee with Jesus, I think of the word *protection*. Psalm 12:7 says, "You, O Lord, will protect us; you will guard us from this generation forever." It is very powerful knowing that we are protected, that we are safe in God's hands.

That does not mean we won't go through trials and tribulations. It does not mean we won't grow old or get sick. But it does mean that we are "divinely" protected. I read a powerful line in a devotional yesterday that said that I am assured wherever I am, God is. When we embrace the presence of God, we have nothing to fear. We can face each day knowing that our protector is with us, and we can handle everything that comes our way.

We cannot say that we trust Jesus and yet live in fear. Today, see all the ways in which God is protecting you! Whatever your fears are, offer them to Him and then let go. There is nothing today that we cannot handle with our Lord and at our side.

Let go and let God…and have a blessed day!

May 6

As I sit, early this morning, having my cup of coffee with Jesus, I was thinking about new life. For months, I have been out on my front porch, and it is amazing to watch the transformation of the trees and the flowers. It reminds me of our own transformation. There are times when we go through deep dark periods and times when we find new life.

Each new day gives us the opportunity for a new life. Each day, we get to choose our own battles, and we get to set our day, either living a new life in Christ or choosing to live in darkness.

So today, choose life.

May 7

As I have coffee with Jesus on this beautiful morning, I can't help but think about mothers. I think of my own mother, who passed away a few years ago. What a gift she was. May is the month of our Blessed Mother, Mary. So this month, I wish all of you who have been mothers a very blessed and Happy Mother's Day.

In a special way, I am thinking of mothers who are estranged from their children or mothers who have lost a child. There are some mothers today who have children who suffer from addiction, from mental illness, or who are, for whatever reason, estranged. I ask you to say a special prayer for your children, to know that they love you, even in their own pain and their own life's journey.

I also lift up mothers who have suffered the loss of a child at any stage of life. I pray that you know the love of your child, the love that can never die. May you live in the promise of Christ that you will be together again. May Mother's Day also remind us of the gift that Christ gave us in His own mother.

Today is a beautiful day to celebrate the gift of our mothers. And I want to thank all the other special women out there who have been mothers to me...you know who you are!

Have a blessed day! And call your mother!

May 8

It's a beautiful morning to have coffee with Jesus. All the reflections I have read this morning all seem to come together today. It says in Philippians 4:13, "I can do all things through Him who strengthens me."

Each day, I hear people grumble, asking what life is all about. The bigger question becomes what are we doing with our lives, with our time, and with our attitudes?

Have you become a better person being challenged? Have you learned a little patience? Have you slowed down from your fast-paced life? And have you grown closer to the Lord? We can do all things through Him who strengthens us, but we need to turn to Him. We may never know all the facts or the true meaning of life. But do we believe God is strengthening us for even greater things?

Today, we have a choice. We can complain about what is going on or we can make this the best day of our lives! It is our choice to bring God's spirit to the forefront. I heard it may be close to one hundred degrees today; we can moan and groan or we can rejoice. But it is what it is, and Jesus has a perfect day planned.

Have a blessed day!

May 9

It is another beautiful morning, having my coffee with Jesus. Deuteronomy 32:3–4 says, "I will proclaim the name of the Lord. O, praise the greatness of our God! He is the Rock, His works are perfect, and His ways are just."

Praise of God is the greatest way to fight anxiety and depression, a way to banish our feelings of fear, doubt, and even our pain. Praising God is not difficult. It just means being aware of His presence and letting yourself go there. You can practice it right now; wherever you are, just look for Him. Just breathe slowly into His presence and feel His safety.

Today, try to praise Him throughout the day. By the way, that even means praising Him when it is one hundred degrees.

May this be a *praising* day.

May 10

As I sit and have my coffee with Jesus, I was thinking about the word *patience*. Yesterday, I was driving, and a car would not let me over into the next lane to exit the off-ramp. Needless to say, I got frustrated. I was waving and had many uncharitable thoughts.

Thirty minutes later, I got back on the freeway going home, and a large truck was trying to move into my lane. I flashed my lights and let him in. He tapped his brakes as if to say, "Thank you." I felt that we created a friendship in that simple action. When I passed him, we waved at each other. I thought this was the way it was supposed to be.

So today, be patient and kind, whether you encounter someone in person or on the road.

Have a blessed day. And drive carefully!

May 11

As I sit and watch the sunrise, and have a cup of coffee with Jesus, I was thinking about the end of life. Last week, I had the gift of visiting with a friend who was dying and who has since passed. She was really in the prime of life and shared with me the importance of time.

She shared that she wished for more time, more time to enjoy the simple things, her family, and her relationships. She had worked a lot and said, "And for what? I have a lot of things, but what I really need is more time." My conversation with her has really challenged me to slow down and focus. I am used to rushing around all day, thinking I am helping people, but now I begin each day with Him, whom I profess to love and serve. This time is not wasted; it has served to put the rest of time in perspective.

Perhaps Jesus is calling you to spend time with Him, time with your spouse and children, time in His creation. Or maybe He is calling you to slow down to experience His presence in this moment. The sun is beginning to rise, and I think of how many of these sunrises I have missed because I was in a hurry. I want to thank my friend for reminding me how precious each moment is.

So take a deep breath. It is a new day. Take time to connect with God, with your family, and with God's creation. Instead of wasting time today, make time for Him!

Or as my mother used to say, "Do not make me give you a time-out!"

Have a blessed day!

May 12

While watching the sunrise, having my coffee with Jesus, I stumbled across a poem. I don't have all of the background about it yet, but it has the initials L.S.P. I felt called to share it with you today.

> The adverse winds
> blew against my life;
> My little ship with grief was tossed.
> My plans were gone—heart full of strife,
> and all my hope seemed to be lost.
> "Then He arose"—one word of peace.
>
> "There was a calm"—a sweet release.
> A tempest great of doubt and fear
> Possessed my mind; no light was there
> To guide or make my vision clear.
> Dark night! 'Twas more than I could be—
> "Then He arose," I saw his face—
> "There was a calm" filled with His grace.
> My heart was sinking 'Neath the wave
> Of deepening test and raging grief;
> All seemed that lost, and then could save,
> And nothing could bring me relief—
> "Then He arose"—and spoke one word,
> "There was a calm!" It Is The Lord!

This day, let us cast our worries and anxieties on the Lord. When we begin this day knowing that we are being held up by our Creator, there is nothing we cannot do.

Have a blessed day!

May 13

This morning, as I was having my cup of coffee with Jesus, I was thinking about graduates. It is the season for graduations. I have grandchildren who are graduating from eighth grade, from high school, and even from college.

I challenge graduates to make a difference, with hearts filled with gratitude! There are so many things you can do to make our world better today.

I challenge my grandchildren and all graduates to write a letter to five people who have made a difference in their lives, telling the parents, grandparents, coaches, and teachers how they helped them get to where they are today. (And be sure and use spellcheck so you sound intelligent!) Or put on your caps and gowns and clean up an elderly person's yard. Or go help serve the homeless in that cap and gown, serenade your grandparents outside their door, drive by your church in your cap and gown and go in, kneel down, and thank God for the blessings you have. My point is that you made it, now share it.

I am so proud of my graduates! I am looking forward to the life they will live, the life that begins today. Put on those caps and gowns, and go out into the world to make a difference. And by the way, take a selfie and send it to me. I would love to celebrate with you.

God bless you!

May 14

As I sit and have my cup of coffee with Jesus, before the sun even rises, I was thinking about news. It's hard today to tell what true news is. I watch different channels, and sometimes, it is hard to know what to believe.

I am not sure if we will ever know all the truth to what is happening in the world, but as Christians, we are given the Good News, the truth! God's Word will lead us through life, for Jesus says, "Come to me, all you who are weary and burdened, and I will give you rest. Take my yoke upon you and learn from me, for I am gentle and humble in heart, and you will find rest for your souls."

That is the only news we need to hear!

So today, let us come to Him and put our trust in His Word!

May 15

Having my late cup of coffee with Jesus this morning, I guess He slept in, or maybe that was me! Either way, we are both here! So I was thinking, do you ever wonder what belongs to you and what belongs to others? I wonder why we spend so much time taking care of what belongs to other people. It could be another person's addiction, or problems, or feelings, or negative behavior. It all belongs to them, and yet sometimes, we try to own it.

People's behaviors are their own, their hopes and dreams are their own, their lies and deceptions are their own, but so often, we want to become their office manager. It is not the job that God assigned to us. We must become our own *life* managers, not everyone else's. We have enough of our own issues and problems ourselves, and we need to own them. We need to take care of them ourselves.

Today, let us work on a clear sense of what belongs to us and let others handle what belongs to them. Today, I will deal with only myself, my issues, and my responsibilities, and I will take my hands off what is not mine. I do this, believing and trusting that God cannot work when I am interfering in someone else's life.

So I am really excited today! I only have to handle my own stuff! Oops, look at that big pile over there…I think it's mine!

Have a blessed day, managing your own life!

May 16

Another beautiful morning watching God's creation come alive while I am having a cup of coffee with Jesus. I have come to find this to be a very important part of my morning. I am used to spending a lot of time organizing my day, my calendar, making my to-do list, and then I try to fit in prayer. Now the first thing I do is sit down with Him, to pray, to listen, and to ask Him to direct my day.

As we create habits, it is important to create habits that drive us to the Father. Yes, that includes physical activity and emotional stability, but most of all, quiet time with Him. Sometimes, self-pity gets in the way. When we become enmeshed in misery, we turn to Him with a list of all the things that are not going right for us. But self-pity removes God from our lives and replaces it with self-interest. It causes us to complain, always wanting more, always wanting answers. We never have enough, we are never satisfied, and then nothing wonderful or amazing can ever happen in our lives.

Today, sit before the King of Kings, take a long, deep breath, and just *be* in His presence. Be in His plan. Be in the moment. That is where it is safe and peaceful and where you will see your Lord.

Have a blessed day!

May 17

As I sit outside, enjoying His handiwork, and having my cup of coffee with Jesus, I was reflecting on *waiting*! Have you ever waited for God to answer a prayer, or asked for Him to show you the way, or asked Him to help you with something, and you felt like He was not listening? He may have been asking you to wait patiently.

Waiting is difficult for most of us. We want things now! We want an answer now! But Jesus tells us that waiting is a gift and that He is preparing us while we wait.

I have been struggling with this for some time. I finally realized that I needed to focus on the waiting itself. As I look back, I do not think I would change this time or anything else that has happened in my life. In my waiting, He has taught me many lessons. He has shown me so clearly His love and presence.

If you are waiting for something from the Lord, know that this waiting time is valuable. Look right in front of you, and you will find what you are looking for. He is speaking to you in the space of *waiting*, and He will show you His love. Psalm 27:14 says, "Wait for the Lord; be strong, and let your heart take courage; wait for the Lord!"

So today, let us strive to be patient, to slow ourselves down, to take a deep breath, and to wait, for He has a perfect plan.

Have a great day!

May 18

As I sit and have my coffee with Jesus, I was thinking about *pressure*. Pressure during difficult times makes us value life. We are better able to understand ourselves and others when things change. When your children go off to college, you are excited, but then you miss them. You cannot wait until they come home, and then, when they do, they just want to be with their friends! And you can't wait for them to go back!

When our lives change, I think about the people who lived through the Great Depression or people who have lived through wars with their loved ones away and in danger, sometimes for many years. In times like that, it is important for us to ask the bigger questions: What do I truly value? What am I doing to make the best of the situation that I have no control over?

When we feel pressure, I know it seems easier to sit and complain, to criticize all those in leadership, to think that they do not know what they are doing, and thereby add to the negative energy that already exists. I challenge you today to find value in this day, in your family, and in the reality that God is ever-present in each moment.

Today, make a difference. A smile and a wave to the people walking their dog, the joy in preparing a meal, the prayers of thanksgiving that we have homes and food and loved ones are all simple ways to cope with daily pressure. We should gain strength from our grandparents and parents who survived much worse than our current problems. Let us value today, because today is all we have, and bring the Spirit of God to all.

Have a blessed day!

May 19

As I sit and have my cup of coffee with Jesus and watch the sunrise, I could not wait to share with you the most exciting news. It is so wonderful, so overwhelming! I just sit here, and I am so full of excitement that I want to shout it from the mountaintops. I am like a kid who has a secret or parents who found out they are having their first child. Each moment the excitement grows, and I just want to share it with someone.

So I am going to share it with you today. Ready? Today is another wonderful day! It was made by God for you and for me, and we should be filled with excitement and joy to be a part of it. It is contagious when you really think about it. Another day of life! Let us enjoy it together. God bless you and have an exciting day.

This is the day the Lord has made, let us rejoice and be glad in it.

May 20

As I sit having my cappuccino with Jesus this morning in Assisi, Italy, I was thinking about peace. We all need to have a place that we go to where we can find the peace of God. For almost fifty years, I have been traveling to Assisi, and every time I come here, I feel at peace.

I also know that, in reality, I can't always be here, so I try to create that feeling again on my front porch, sitting in church, or while walking my dog, Francis.

So today, find a moment to sit in the peace of Christ, no matter where you are. Go to your peaceful place, if you can. But if you can't, just close your eyes, go to that special place in your mind, and spend a moment with Jesus. Let him give you the peace that is beyond all understanding.

Have a blessed day! Ciao!

May 21

As I sit and have my cup of coffee with Jesus and wait for the sun to rise, I was reflecting on how many people suffer from anxiety and depression and how hard it sometimes is for their families and friends. I do not know if I really understood depression until this last year, but I have come to believe that it is very *real*. I have found trying to focus on positive things and counting my blessings helps me to get through those difficult days.

The problem is, when you are going through depression, others do not always understand. They think you should just be able to snap out of it. But like so many other illnesses, it is usually a very private and silent thing. Do not be ashamed if you feel depressed! You are not alone! Just know that we are members of the same club.

Maybe you do not suffer from depression, but I guarantee you, there is somebody in your life who does! Pray for them, walk with them, and make sure that you are patient with them. I still have very strong bouts of depression! It seems that every time I do, Jesus reaches out and takes my hand; I realize he carried me through another day. And tomorrow will be a new day filled with light.

I find that turning to the scriptures, sharing with people you can trust, or seeing a therapist if you must can all help bring you out of the darkness. Depression is not necessarily a club I would choose to join, but I have certainly met amazing people who have taught me how to keep moving forward and keep focused on the *light*.

I know that Jesus is the light! I believe that is why Jesus came into the world as the *light*, to clear the darkness. Today is going to be an amazing day because I will walk in the light.

Have a wonderful day.

May 22

As I sit and have my cup of coffee with Jesus, I looked up and found Francis, my dog, was sitting on the chair. It made me think of what a wonderful gift pets are. They are those special creatures that teach us unconditional love.

When we give praise to God for the blessings in our lives, very seldom do we offer everything to Him, including companions like Francis. The way my dog is excited to greet me when I come home, the way he comes to lay his head on my chest when he knows I am sad, when he pushes me to play when I do not feel like playing, all shows me how animals are one of God's special blessings.

The special thing about Francis is that he loves me just the way I am—no judgment, no criticism, just unconditional love. This love mirrors the love that God has for me. Maybe there is a lot we can learn from the gift of the pet companions that God has given us. It seems we are always trying to teach our pets new tricks, while they are trying to teach us life lessons. I cherish these special gifts that God gives me; I give Him praise for all pets.

Today, I give thanks to God for the gift of Francis and the many pets I've had before. And today, I think I will watch and learn. I still haven't figured out how to roll over and surrender!

Have a blessed day, and spend some time with your pet.

May 23

As I sit out front and have my cup of coffee and a scone from a friend with Jesus, I was thinking about *treasures*. *Jesus Calling*, a book of reflections, spoke about treasures. Two of my readings today spoke of treasures, and yesterday, my six-year-old grandson came over and made a treasure hunt for me. He took Stick-Ups and posted them around the yard. I had to find the *treasure*, which was a note that said, "I love you."

Every day, we are on a treasure hunt! Just like the game with my grandson, we need to slow ourselves down and quiet ourselves to see the *treasures* that Jesus has in store for us today. I have a list of things to do, some projects I want to get done, but I do not want to miss the treasure hunt Jesus has waiting for me today!

Today, I am going to try to focus on the *treasures* that God has hidden for me to find and be grateful that, in the end, they lead to the great "I love you!" As I sit here, I see a blue jay in the front yard, and I hear other birds that are singing very loudly and neighbors walking by and waving. I have a list of people to pray for, and I have a scone. It is a brand-new day!

Have a blessed day!

May 24

As I sit out on my porch this beautiful morning, having a cup of coffee with Jesus, I was thinking how important our attitude about *life* is! During times of trouble, it is easy to wonder what there is to do, to feel confined, to want your old life back!

Life is not meant to be endured, life is to be enjoyed and embraced! We all go through trials and tribulations, but life can be exciting if we strive to live in the present moment. When life slows down, people tend to dwell on the past or get nervous for the future, and they miss the *present*.

As I sit here, I try to move my mind from the "should've been" or the "might've been" or the "maybe it will happen" to be *present* in this very moment. This moment is perfect, and I am here, and God is here. I must embrace what is instead of merely enduring.

I know that God will bring me some *sacred* interruptions (that is what I call situations, people, and plans I did not count on today), and I will embrace them. Today, Jesus and I may have a second cup of coffee. I think I want to embrace this moment.

Have a blessed day!

May 25

As I have my cup of coffee with Jesus and read my reflections, I am stuck on the word *if*. How often do we use that word *if*? I would have done this or that *if* this had happened in my life, *if* things had turned out differently. *If* always takes us to the past. Jesus calls us to live in the present, to *be*!

I love these moments in the morning, because they allow me to *be* with Him, to breathe in the newness of life, and hope, and peace. When I live in the *if*, I am agitated, frustrated, and cannot find peace. To *be* is not a far place to travel to, it is just *present*, in this moment.

It is here that we encounter the Sacred Heart of Jesus, the mystery of our faith, the *present*...His *presence*.

Today, I am going to strive to *be*, and *if* I do not, that is my own doing. My first thought is I wonder *if* it is going to be one hundred degrees here today! Negativity and dread already! So I changed my thinking; it is going to *be* at least one hundred degrees? See how easy that is?

Have a wonderful day!

May 26

As I sit to have my cup of coffee with Jesus, and watch the sun come up, I was thinking about *friendship*. You never really know who your true friends are until you go through a difficult time. Jesus wants to be *our* friend. He has invited us into a personal relationship, based on *love, mercy, and forgiveness*!

To build a relationship with anyone requires the desire to spend time with them. With time, the relationship builds trust and vulnerability. To build our relationship with Jesus, we need to study His Word, experience Him in the sacraments, and spend time alone with Him in prayer and meditation.

Over the past few years, I have grown in my relationship with Christ by taking this simple time every morning to turn to Him! He has taught me so much. Today, Jesus invites *you* into that same relationship. Pour yourself a cup of coffee, get out your Bible, and sit back and get to know Him! He *is waiting*. I think He likes a strong caramel macchiato or at least I know I do!

Have a blessed day!

May 27

Today, as I sit and have my cup of coffee with Jesus, I read that we had a small earthquake last night. I slept right through it. People have been posting things like, "That's all we need." I started to look for the locus, but all I could find were mosquitoes this morning!

We were not created to live in fear. We were created to love and trust our Lord. The power of God protects us. In Psalm 12:7, it says, "You, O Lord, will protect us; you will guard us from this generation forever." I trust in His Word and in His promises!

Today, I am going to choose to make this a wonderful day. Even with one hundred ten degrees weather, earthquakes, and mosquitoes, it becomes a *choice*. I can make the best of today and count my blessings! I can be positive, affirming, and kind, or I can complain, be critical, and sad. Is it not great that we have a choice? With Jesus on our side, it makes life a lot easier. Put a little sunscreen on and some mosquito repellent, keep your feet on solid ground, and stay in the shade. It is going to be a wonderful day.

Blessings, and if the ground shakes again, make it a dance.

May 28

As I sit and have my daily cup of coffee with Jesus, I was reflecting on the power and gift of *forgiveness*. Forgiveness is very difficult for me, but having a relationship with Jesus does not make it an *option*! Often, it is easier to accept God's forgiveness or the forgiveness of others than it is to forgive ourselves. But forgiveness sets us free!

I know neighbors, families, or even congregations that have fallen apart because of the lack of forgiveness. Good friendships have ended, marriages and businesses have collapsed, often due to a lack of forgiveness. People believe that forgiveness means you forget. Not true! I believe *forgiveness* means you move forward. In Colossians 3:13, the Bible says, "Bear with each other and forgive whatever grievances you may have against one another. Forgive as the Lord forgives you!"

When we pay back people by withholding forgiveness, we are really doing damage to ourselves. But when we forgive, "We set the prisoner free and then we discover that the prisoner was *us*," from the book, *The Art of Forgiving*, by Lewis Smedes.

Today is a great day for us to set ourselves free, to *forgive*. Think of someone who has wronged you. Ask God for the grace to let it go and then breathe in His love and His forgiveness! Jesus says that we must forgive seventy times seven. Yuck, I need to go now. I have a lot of forgiving to do!

It is going to be a wonderful day. Blessings!

May 29

As I sit and have my cup of coffee with Jesus, I was thinking about grieving. Grief is a difficult task to undertake. Yesterday, one of my friends went to see the Lord. Father Larry was a priest for over fifty years and spent the last twenty-eight years coming to my parishes, celebrating both Easter and Christmas, and spent a month in the summer (takes a special friend to come to Bakersfield in June and July!). He spent his life in Catholic education, but most of all, he had a deep and close relationship with our Lord.

I will miss our Sunday night talks, the holidays, the traveling, and the summers. I will miss my friend. But I also sit out daily talking with our Lord, dreaming of that time that I see Jesus face-to-face.

I know there are stages of grieving. I have watched them and been through this before. Today, I am going to choose to celebrate my friend! I am having a second cup of coffee with Jesus and thanking Him for the years he gave me with him. I am going to reflect on his new life with our Lord, a life that he worked so hard for. I am going to lift up his family, the Marianist community, and all the lives he impacted. And I say, "Well done, my good and faithful servant, go and share your Master's reward." And you would be very proud of your family: they think of you every day, they feel your presence, and they trust in God.

Have a blessed day!

May 30

As I sit on this beautiful morning and have my cup of coffee with Jesus, I feel myself growing uneasy. The newspaper headlines show protests and riots throughout our country. Two homeless people just passed by asking for water. It makes me feel that there is a negative energy in the universe.

I do not want to add to that negativity, so I sit here and ask the Lord to fill me with His Holy Spirit. During the vigil of Pentecost, the world received the gift of God's Spirit in a special way. I know that His Spirit is stronger than all this negativity energy, and if we, as a universe, can join with His Spirit, things will change.

Today, I am going to intentionally call upon His Spirit, not only to enter my heart, but to pulsate out into the world so that the world may know the power and *love* of God. Can you imagine what would happen if each one of us was to allow the spirit of God to flow from us today? If we could just get out of our own minds and *be* present in the moment, we could change our world.

Come, Holy Spirit, come renew the face of the earth.

Come, Holy Spirit, come within me.

Come, Holy Spirit, come and bring to the world the love of God.

Have a blessed day!

May 31

As I sit and have my cup of coffee with Jesus on this beautiful morning, I am reflecting on a quote I read from Mrs. Charles Cowman's book, *Streams in the Desert*. It says, "The meaning of trial is not only to test worthiness but to increase it; the oak is not only tested by the storms, but it is toughened by them."

When we are forced to deal with death of someone we care about and love, we are also forced to see the pain. This can be overwhelming, for love and pain often go hand in hand. You cannot love your spouse for seventy years, like a friend did, and not experience the pain of his passing. Pain and love go together. Another friend shared something she read about childbirth, that the pain of delivery goes away when that child is held by its parents for the first time.

Whatever trials we feel we are going through right now, we need to focus. Trials make us rethink the way we were living. They make us slow down, force us to spend more time with our family, and recognize the simple things of life. Trials can make us stronger, more creative, and hopefully, more spiritual.

So if we can embrace the trials we have and trust that they are making us stronger (like the oak), we grow closer to God. He is preparing us for a new earth, a new life, where pain and love will explode together, where the universe will finally be at peace, and all will come to be one with God.

So when you embrace the pain of whatever trial you're going through today, don't ignore the love that came with that pain. Remember, the cross brought about the resurrection. You can handle it. You are not alone. He sent the Holy Spirit to show you the way.

Have a blessed day, and may the Spirit of God be with you.

June 1

As I sit and have my cup of coffee with Jesus, I was thinking of how many people have told me recently that they feel *overwhelmed*. Sometimes life can happen very fast and we feel attacked by many different facets of life. That's when we need to stay centered on Jesus.

People sometimes say He never gives us more than we can handle. I would really like to know who those people are! When we do feel overwhelmed, it's important for us to get centered, to *breathe*, and to realize that everything is in Jesus's hands. The only reason we feel overwhelmed is because we are taking responsibility for something God never intended us to take responsibility for. In the end, we cannot control everything that comes our way, and we certainly cannot control others.

If we sit for a moment, close our eyes, take a deep breath, and surrender our worry and anxiety to Him, we will realize that we are *okay*. We can get through anything with Him. Try not to be overwhelmed and know that He is there to defend you, to comfort you, and to assure you that everything is part of His perfect plan.

Have a wonderful day, and be *overwhelmed* by His *love!*

June 2

As I sit and have my cup of coffee with Jesus, I was thinking about the word *caring*. To me, caring is concern for someone or caring about a cause or about things we love or things that we put ahead of ourselves. When we go out of our way to be caring, we always feel good, because that's when we resemble Jesus the most.

Don't get me wrong. We also need to have self-care and take care of ourselves. But to truly find joy and happiness, caring for others needs to be an essential part of our daily life.

Today, find someone that you can reach out to and be caring. Maybe just a phone call or a text or even just a kind word. If our entire world became more caring, we would find the peace and love that Christ intended.

Have a blessed and caring day!

June 3

As I sit and have my cup of coffee with Jesus, I am reflecting on the Surrender Novena, given to us by Jesus to Fr. Dolindo Ruotolo (1882–1970…you can Google it). I have prayed it every day now for the past two years, and each day, it feels like a brand-new prayer. Today, I repeat Day 4, which says, "Do not worry; close your eyes, and say to Me with faith: 'Thy will be done.' You take care of it. And I say to you that I will take care of it, and that I will intervene as a doctor; and I will accomplish miracles when they are needed." Then comes *the* most powerful prayer, "O, Jesus, I surrender myself to You. You take care of everything."

When you feel overwhelmed or experience fear or anxiety, pray this prayer. Surrender what you cannot control so that Jesus can be the true Lord of your life. Every day, I begin with this Surrender Prayer, trusting that Jesus hears me and is working in my life.

Today, experience the presence of Jesus in the moment, in each experience, and in each person He brings you. Living in His presence and surrendering to Him will make this the best day of your life.

Have a blessed day, and give it all to Him.

June 4

It is another beautiful morning, having coffee with Jesus. All of the reflections I am reading this morning seem to come together today. In Philippians 4:13, it says, "I can do all things through Him who strengthens me." Each day, we struggle not to complain, and I wonder if it really matters. It just is what it is!

The bigger question becomes what we are doing with it...with our time, our attitudes? Have we become better people when challenged? Have we learned a little patience? Have we slowed down from our fast-paced lives? And have we grown closer to the Lord?

We can do all things through Him who strengthens us, but we need to turn to Him. We may never know all the facts, we may have done things differently, but what are we doing today? Do we believe God is strengthening us for even greater things?

Today, we have a choice. We can complain about what's going on or we can make this the best day of our lives! It is our choice to bring God's spirit to the forefront.

I heard it may be close to one hundred degrees today. We can moan and groan, or we can rejoice. But it is what it is, and Jesus has a perfect day planned for us.

Have a blessed day!

June 5

As I sit and have my cup of coffee with Jesus, I am thinking about the word *energy*. From the time my eyes open in the morning until the end of the day, my *energy* level changes. Have you ever met someone who drains you of your energy because of all their drama? On the same note, have you ever met someone whose energy is so contagious that they lift your spirit?

As Christians, our *energy* (or spirit) needs to flow from our relationship with Christ. This is what made the disciples so dynamic. The Spirit of Christ was the *energy* that flowed out of them.

How is your energy level today? Are you tired or overwhelmed, angry or sad? Then it's time to reconnect with our Lord and allow His *energy* to lift you up. Today, become energized by the one who created you and who loves you. And then take that *energy* and *spirit* and spread it to our world. There is only one kind of real *energy*, and that is *energy* that comes from the Father, through the Son, in the Holy Spirit.

Have a blessed day!

June 6

As I sit and have my cup of coffee with Jesus, I was thinking about the need to RESIST NEGATIVITY. Do you notice how some people carry a deep spirit of negativity with them? The negativity might be pent up anger, or a lack of forgiveness, or painful emotions.

It's easy to be pulled into that negativity. Sometimes, even as we try to be POSITIVE, that negative energy force throws us off balance. We have to be careful not to be pulled into that darkness. It does neither of us any good. To help someone come to the LIGHT, we do NOT have to step into their darkness. Be the LIGHT. Allow the light of Christ to shine through you.

Today, I'm going to be aware of the negativity that lies deep in the lives of the people I love, and, instead of trying to fix them, I'm going to be the LIGHT. I am going to allow the LIGHT of Christ to shine through me.

Have a blessed day!

June 7

As I sit and have my cup of coffee with Jesus, I was thinking about the word GENEROUS. Have you ever met someone who is, by nature, generous? People who sometimes share what they have, sometimes share good advice, or sometimes just offer a listening ear are Generous.

Scriptures tell us in Proverbs 11:25, "A generous person will prosper; whoever refreshes others will be refreshed." And 2 Corinthians 9:11 says, "You will be enriched in every way so that you can be GENEROUS on every occasion, and through us, your generosity will result in thanksgiving to God."

GENEROSITY, then, becomes a prayer. Today is a good day to examine your own sense of generosity and then compare it to GOD'S generosity to you. Would people say that you are GENEROUS with your gifts? If you're like me, you know you have a lot of work to do!

Have a blessed day!

June 8

As I sit and have my cup of coffee with Jesus, I was thinking about *time*. This morning, when I looked at my clock, it was 4:05 a.m. And I thought that 4:05 a.m. is the only time that I will have this very moment. There will never ever be another exact 4:05 a.m. today. What if I could see all *time* like that, knowing that no moment will ever repeat itself? And I have the ability to be present and joyful in this very moment.

I have been watching the TV series called *The Chosen*. (I highly recommend it.) In it, I have noticed that Jesus is always present in the moment. He takes advantage of each moment, not manipulating it, but rather living it to its fullest.

So this is our challenge, to wake up with a smile, to be grateful for the moments that we will never experience again, and to be present. You will never have another day like today, this day, so why not make it the best day ever? Put a smile on your face and get excited about all that God has planned for you today.

Have a blessed day!

June 9

I am out early this morning, having my cup of coffee with Jesus. And I realize how important it is that I have a positive attitude before Him in prayer. During these times, it seemed easy to have negative thoughts, like what day is it? Or what am I going to do today? And you can find yourself going into a negative place.

But when you put your mind on Jesus, it is easy to turn things around. Our thoughts become focused on what a glorious day this is! I can't wait to see what God brings to me to carry out today!

Today, I am going to mindfully be aware of how *big* and good our God is. I'm going to mindfully see Him in the beauty of His creation and mindfully listen for His voice. In the end, everything in life is a choice, and I am going to choose today to be *positive*, loving, forgiving, and happy. I wonder if people will even recognize me!

Join me today, and bring that gift of God's love, His positive energy, into our world.

Have a blessed day.

June 10

As I sit and have my cup of coffee with Jesus, I was reflecting on Matthew 28:20, "I am with you always." Those are amazing and powerful words, especially if you are going through a difficult time. Maybe you are having difficulty in your relationship, your finances, your health, or maybe you are just full of anxiety. That is when you need to reflect on those words.

It is powerful to realize we are never alone, to know that we are loved, to know that we are forgiven. This is the powerful promise that our Lord gives us.

So if you're frustrated, hurt, angry, or worried, just reflect on the words of Jesus, who says, "I am with you always," and know that you are in good hands.

Today is a new day. Jesus wants to walk with you. All you need to do is invite Him in.

Have a blessed day. I know He is there with you!

June 11

As I sit and have my cup of coffee with Jesus, I was thinking about GRIEF. I spoke with a number of people in the last few weeks who have experienced the loss of loved ones. When we recall that pain, we experience GRIEF. One of my friends shared a quote they found that says, "And when nobody wakes you up in the morning, and when nobody waits for you at night, and when you can do whatever you want, what do you call it, freedom or loneliness?"

That is a lot to think about, because whenever there is loss, there is great change. I think that when we are in grief, our emotions go back-and-forth. Every situation is a little different, but the effects of GRIEF are profound!

Another quote I've found is, "GRIEF is just love with nowhere to go!" If you, or someone you know, are experiencing grief, then turn to our Lord! Let HIM embrace you and your uncertainty, for Jesus says, "Come to me, all you who are weary, and I will give you rest."

Today, reach out to a friend who may be grieving. Or, if you yourself are grieving, spend some time with the Lord and feel his comforting embrace.

Have a blessed day!

June 12

As I sit and have my cup of coffee with Jesus, I was thinking about the words *overcoming fear*. Fear is so debilitating. I realize that, for much of my life, I have lived in fear. I was afraid of making mistakes, fear of the dark, or fear that somebody wouldn't like me. So many things to fear.

When we live in fear, we cannot live in the trust and grace of the Father. We either put our hope and trust in Him or in the world, where fear is produced. If you're tired of being afraid of people or situations in your life or even of life itself, then it's time to turn back to the Father.

God has led me through a wild journey from fear to trust. Today, I am not afraid! It says in Romans 8:31–32, "If God is for us, who is against us?" He who did not withhold His own Son, but rather, gave Him up for all of us. Will He not also give us everything else?

Today, remember that with Jesus, we have nothing to fear! Jesus came here that we might have life and have it abundantly!

Have a blessed day, replacing fear with trust!

June 13

As I sit and have my cup of coffee with Jesus, I am thinking about the word FREEDOM. Epictetus said, "But anyone who can be restricted, coerced, or pushed into something against what they will is a slave." The Bible tells us in Galatians 5:1, "It is for freedom that Christ has set us free. Stand firm, then, and do not let yourselves be a burden again by a yoke of slavery." And Psalm 119:45 says, "I will walk about in freedom, for I have sought out your precepts."

It is good for us to reflect on freedom, that we have choices, and that our choices should be guided by God's WORD. We can feel controlled, or have our freedoms taken away by others, but true freedom comes from Christ and our relationship with HIM. It allows us to live and preach the GOOD NEWS.

Today, embrace the freedom that Jesus called you to. Live in freedom, not controlled, coerced, or restricted, but in the true freedom of faith. It is liberating to live in Christ's freedom.

Let the GOOD NEWS of Jesus Christ live through you!

June 14

As I sit and have my cup of coffee with Jesus, I was thinking about the word PROMISE. Have you ever made a promise to God and then not kept it? I think, over the course of my life, there were many times I tried to bargain with God or make promises to Him. Even carrying out my Lenten PROMISES is hard! The powerful thing is, that though I may fail in keeping my PROMISES to the LORD, HE never fails to keep HIS promises to me.

Jesus's PROMISES are real. He doesn't promise us fame, wealth, or riches, but HE does PROMISE us joy, peace, and understanding. John 15:9 says, "As the Father has loved me, so I have loved you. Now remain in My love." His promise to love us and to be our light is HIS gift. Studying and reading the scriptures helps us to remain in HIS love, and to learn and embrace HIS promises. HE is faithful!

Today, I am going to reflect on HIS PROMISES and remember that the closer I stay to HIM, the better I can live out my promise to serve HIM. Isn't it great to know we have someone in our lives who always keeps His promises?!

Have a blessed day!

June 15

As I sit and have my cup of coffee with Jesus, I was thinking about the word *consistency*. *Consistency* means acting or doing something in the same way over time. Scripture tells us in Hebrews 13:8, "Jesus Christ is the same yesterday and today and forever." I think it is important that we have consistency in our lives, consistency in the way in which we live, consistency in our prayer lives, and especially, consistency in our relationship with the Lord!

I was thinking about things I'm consistent with, and I was reminded today that I have posted Coffee with Jesus for over 360 consecutive days. I sometimes wish I was as consistent with my workouts and my diet!

Today, I am going to strive to be more consistent in my walk with the Lord, taking time for real prayer, for silence, and for listening to the direction of his spirit.

Have a blessed day!

June 16

As I sit and have my cup of coffee with Jesus, I was thinking of the word *competition*. I don't think I have ever thought of myself as a competitive person, but then realize I am.

My eight-year-old grandson came over the other day and got out the chessboard. He was determined to beat me, and I was determined to beat him. He would make a move that surprised me, and then I would checkmate him. What I found during our competition was that we never laughed so hard! We spent a wonderful afternoon in friendly competition.

So competition isn't always bad. Let's remember that the greatest gift of competition is not to win, but to quote my grandson, "Have fun!"

Have a blessed day!

June 17

As I sit and have my cup of coffee with Jesus, I was thinking of the word *disappointment*. When I think of disappointment, I usually think immediately of the people who are disappointed in me. But today, I was thinking about people I may have disappointed. Have I disappointed my children or my grandchildren? Who else have I disappointed?

My parents lived with me before they passed. Was I patient enough? Did I do everything I could to ease their last days? And in dealing with people who come to talk to me, have I been compassionate and understanding enough?

I don't think we need to dwell on who we may have disappointed or who may have disappointed us, but it doesn't hurt to sometimes look and see how we can be more loving, forgiving, and merciful.

Have a blessed day.

June 18

As I sit and have my cup of coffee with Jesus, I was thinking about the word CLOSURE. Someone sent me a quote the other day that said, "If the door CLOSES, quit banging on it! Whatever was behind it wasn't meant for you. Consider the fact that maybe the door was CLOSED because you were worth so much more than what was on the other side."

Throughout our lives, we have moments where there is CLOSURE. It could be the death of someone we love, the end of a marriage, a change in our occupation, or even things like depression and anxiety. Sometimes we need to take a good look at our lives and not be afraid to CLOSE the door that brings pain and open the one that brings us new beginnings. It's amazing how many doors keep opening. I think that must be how Jesus works.

Today, try not to see closure as something negative, but rather as something exciting. I used to love the TV show, "Let's Make a Deal"...I always wanted to know what was behind Door Number Two!

Have a great day and just watch as new doors open. And be sure to let the Spirit of God lead you.

June 19

As I sit and have my cup of coffee with Jesus, I am filled with *gratitude*. In the month of June, we celebrate Father's Day. I was blessed to have had a wonderful father, who served as a great example of what it means to sacrifice for your children. I was also blessed forty years ago to adopt my first child and now have eight who consider me their father.

The title of *father* is not something that someone gives you. It is an honor that has to be earned. Anybody can bring a child into the world, but it takes a special man to be a *father*. I look at my sons with pride and thanks, for they are all amazing *fathers*. And I thank the many men I have met in my life who were and are true fathers.

So today, I ask God to bless all of you. Though not everyone had a wonderful father in their lives, God the Father is always there for each one of us. Let us remember our fathers, living and deceased, and thank God for them, and for the gift of being called *father* ourselves!

Have a blessed day!

June 20

As I sit and have my cup of coffee with Jesus, I was thinking about being *calm*. So often in life, I get anxious about things, and I sometimes allow those things to overrun me. I have to consciously rein myself in.

And then there are occasions when I deal with life calmly. My grandson told me he feels calm when he plays video games. For me, it's taking a deep breath or sometimes simply looking out at nature and feeling the presence of Christ. When we are calm and in the presence of God, we can handle anything.

So today, take a deep breath. Look at God's creation or play a video game, and find the place where you can be calm.

Have a calm, blessed day.

June 21

As I sit and have my cup of coffee with Jesus, I was thinking of the word *kindness*. Kindness is an action word. Every day, we are given the opportunity to be kind. Practicing the art of kindness gives me the opportunity to share my gifts and talents and to be Christ to others.

I saw a post on Facebook the other day. My grandson was helping his little cousin climb up on a bounce house. I thought what a simple act of kindness that small gesture was; it went a long way. You could see the big smile on her face, even in the post.

Kindness doesn't always have to be a big act. Sometimes, the simplest ones bring the greatest joy. So be kind today.

Have a blessed day.

June 22

As I sit and have my cup of coffee with Jesus, I was thinking about the word *sparkle*. I actually met a young woman who is a caregiver, and her name is Sparkle…really!

Every time I see something that sparkles, it draws my attention, whether it be a star at night, the bling that so many people wear, or this young woman named Sparkle. She just sparkles! Her love and compassion for people in the last stages of their lives is truly amazing. You can feel Jesus flowing through her.

Today, let us be conscious that we, too, need to sparkle. We need to bring that light of Christ into our world in any way we can. And I thank God for people like Sparkle, who remind us of that gift.

Have a blessed day. And don't forget to sparkle!

June 23

As I sit and have my cup of coffee with Jesus, I was thinking about ANGER. In the past few days, a number of people have shared with me the anger they are feeling. They have either been hurt by someone or are frustrated with what's happening in their lives. Sometimes they don't even know what they are angry about.

I have learned over the years that ANGER only destroys the person who holds onto it. We need to examine our lives and be truthful about why we are angry. Most of the time, it's about our own choices.

Isn't it wonderful that we have a God who does not hold grudges or remains angry, but continually challenges us to be more focused on HIM, rather than on holding on to anger?

Sometimes that is easier said than done. The scriptures tell us in James 1:19-20, "Know this, my beloved brothers: let every person be quick to hear, slow to speak, slow to anger; for the anger of man does not produce the righteousness of God."

Today, if you're angry with someone, or at some situation, or even with yourself, ask God to help you let it go and focus on HIS love and mercy. And watch the anger dissipate.

Have a blessed day!

June 24

As I sit on my patio, saying my morning prayers and having a cup of coffee with Jesus, I was reflecting on the verse from Matthew 28:20, "I am with you always." What amazing and powerful words, especially when we are going through difficult times. With many people out of work, worried about finances, or some overworking and just stressed about life in general, listen to Him. "I am with you always."

To know that we are never alone, to know that we are loved, to know that we are forgiven, this is the most powerful promise that our Lord has ever given us.

Today, whether you are feeling happy, frustrated, depressed, or just worried, listen to Jesus, who says to you, "I am with you always," and know that you are in good hands. It is a new day to walk with him.

Have a great day!

June 25

As I sit and have my cup of coffee with Jesus, I was thinking about the word *protection*. Psalm 12:7 says, "You, O Lord, will protect us; you will guard us from this generation forever." Isn't it powerful to know that we are *protected*, that we are safe in God's hands?

Being *protected* does not mean that we won't go through trials and tribulations. It doesn't mean that we won't grow old or get sick, but it does mean that we are *divinely* protected. We are assured that, wherever we are, God is with us! When we embrace His presence, we have nothing to fear. We cannot say that we trust Jesus and yet live in fear.

So today, try to see all the ways in which God is *protecting* you! Whatever your fears are, offer them to Him and then let go. There is nothing today that we cannot handle with our Lord at our side. Let go and let God!

Have a blessed day!

June 26

As I sit and have my cup of coffee with Jesus, I was thinking about the word *excitement*. It seems like it has been a long time since people have been *excited* about anything. The other day, a friend said to me, "The only thing I am excited about is going to bed at night and saying goodbye to a nothing day."

As Christians, we should be *excited* about many things. We should be excited about each new day and the many ways in which God speaks to us. We should be excited that as a community, we can work through many obstacles. We should be excited about God's Word and know that we are not alone, that there is a divine plan.

So it's time to wake up and get *excited*. It's time to stop complaining about what was and be excited about what *is*. Just think, we have a whole day to see God's hand at work. We have the choice to be *excited* or *bored*. I've decided I'm going choose to be *excited* today!

Have a blessed and exciting day!

June 27

As I sit and have my cup of coffee with Jesus, I was thinking about *perseverance* in *prayer*. I was studying the words of Elijah when I discovered what a powerful prayer he created. It was bold and full of confidence. Elijah did not beat around the bush or even bargain with God. He believed in God's promises, and he prayed with authority.

In studying 1 Kings 18:20–40, Elijah tells us that we do not need to pray in secret; rather, we need to be bold and strong when we pray. God tells us to come boldly into His presence. This is very powerful, because we are followers of Jesus Christ, and we can believe and trust in His promises.

Today, I am going to pray *boldly* to my God. I am going to trust His promises to me and pray with confidence for people and situations where I need His guidance.

So whatever you were praying about, pray with *perseverance and confidence*! Trust that God hears you and will keep His promises.

Have a blessed day!

June 28

As I sit and have my cup of coffee with Jesus, I was thinking about things that we *hand over*. We talk about *handing over* our life to Jesus. And that is a good thing.

However, sometimes, I think we *hand over* our minds to many other entities. We *hand over* our minds to our cell phones, to television, to social media. We even let other people tell us what we should be doing, what we should look like, or what we should be thinking! Most of the time, we aren't even aware that we are doing this. We are mindlessly handing over our lives! We do not let the world control our bodies, and we should not let it control our minds!

Today, I am going to think for myself and limit the time I look at my phone. I am going to let the Lord speak to me instead of listening to the ramblings of the world. I am going to *hand over* my mind to the Lord.

Have a great, free, and blessed day!

June 29

As I sit and have my cup of coffee with Jesus, I was thinking about a phrase I read in one of my daily reflections, called "CROSS BEARERS FOR CHRIST." What a powerful phrase! Each of us is called to be a CROSS BEARER!

Being a CROSS BEARER means to take action, to use our brokenness for service, to not be afraid to get into the arena. We hear in scripture, Matthew 16:24-26, "If anyone wishes to come after ME, He must deny himself, and take up his cross and follow ME."

Many people sat back and watched Jesus go by, but Simon of Cyrene and Veronica took action. The world will always remember them because Simon of Cyrene helped Jesus carry the cross. And we will remember Veronica for her courage and kindness in wiping the face of Jesus.

We all have CROSSES TO BEAR, and we need each other to help to carry them. Today, think of friends who need help carrying the cross and become a CROSS BEARER. Call them, visit them, enter into their passion, and be a friend. What a beautiful world it would be if we helped each other carry our crosses.

Have a blessed day!

June 30

As I sit and have my cup of coffee with Jesus, I was thinking about the word PRAISE. The dictionary says PRAISE is the expression of approval or admiration for someone or something. Every morning, we need to wake up and PRAISE God, for we have been given the chance for a new day, a new beginning.

And the scriptures often remind us about PRAISE. We need to praise God in good times and in bad. David says in Psalm 68:19, "PRAISE be to the Lord, the God our Savior, who daily bears our burdens."

To PRAISE is to give thanks. Deuteronomy 7:9, says, "I PRAISE you, God, for you keep your covenant of love to a thousand generations of those who love you and keep your commandments."

We PRAISE God for life, and we even praise HIM for the trials we endure! Remember, PRAISE is the highest form of prayer.

So today, PRAISE the Lord, and have a blessed day!

July 1

As I sit and have my cup of coffee with Jesus, I was thinking of the word PERSEVERE. There is a difference between perseverance and endurance. Perseverance consists of having an absolute trust in what is going to happen. To PERSEVERE through any hardship is built on trust that there is nothing to fear.

Jesus stood for love, peace, justice, forgiveness, and mercy. To PERSEVERE means that we believe in all of this and that we will not be let down because Jesus is always at our side.

There may be moments in our life we experience disappointment, challenges, and even suffering, but through it all we remain faithful to God's promises. We want to be like Saint Timothy, who said, "I fought the good fight. I finished the race. I kept the faith!"

Today, PERSEVERE with joy and peace. Be a true witness that Jesus is the Lord of your life!

Have a blessed day!

July 2

As I sit and have my cup of coffee with Jesus, I was thinking about the word KINDNESS. Ephesians 4:32 says, "Be kind to one another, tenderhearted, forgiving one another, as God in Christ forgave you."

Yesterday I witnessed so many acts of KINDNESS. From breakfast in the morning with a priest friend and all the people that came up to me, to lunch at Woolgrowers, the waitress, all the people and of course Jenny, I experienced KINDNESS. I visited a few friends who are very ill and the KINDNESS their caregivers were showing was beautiful. Colossians 3:12 says, "Put on then, as GOD'S chosen ones, holy and beloved, compassionate hearts, KINDNESS, humility, meekness and patience."

Can you imagine what our world would be like if we all did simple acts of KINDNESS? Let us strive to follow the words of Mother Teresa who said, "We can do no great things-only small things with great love."

Today, be aware of the tone in your voice, all of the occasions that God gives you to share KINDNESS, and act on it. As we show KINDNESS, we show GOD!

Have a blessed and kind day!

July 3

As I sit and have my cup of coffee with Jesus, I was thinking of the word *choice*. Every day of our lives, we make choices. I wish I could say we always make good *choices*, but if we make a bad choice, we are blessed to have faith and another chance to make things new.

Today, as we wake up, we can make a *choice* as to how we're going to live. We can begin by dedicating our day to serving Christ or we can choose to work on our to-do list. We need to think often about the *choices* we make, and we need to include Jesus in them. We can *choose* to put a smile on our faces and greet people with joy, or we can be negative all day. We can *choose* to see the beauty of God's creation, or we can spend the day complaining.

Isn't it a wonderful gift that we get to *choose*? Today, I am going to *choose* to make this a day of joy, love, and forgiveness. I am going to *choose* to put a smile on my face and celebrate a new day! What a great day to be grateful and to *choose* to make the world a better place.

Have a blessed day!

July 4

As I sit and have my cup of coffee this morning with Jesus, I was thinking about *freedom*. It is sometimes easy to take our freedoms for granted. Our freedom of speech, freedom of religion, freedom from fear, and freedom from want. Today is a great day to reflect on the freedoms we enjoy and to remember those who continue to uphold our freedoms.

In a special way today, I want to remember our brave servicemen and women who continually protect and defend our freedoms. And there are others who defend our freedoms, those who serve in law enforcement, the firefighters who protect our homes, educators who instill in our children reverence for our nation and respect for others, and those who inspire faith in our country's institutions.

Today is a day to remember and give thanks to God for our country and for our way of life.

Have a wonderful and happy Fourth of July!

July 5

As I sit and have my cup of coffee with Jesus, I was thinking about the word NEW. Don't you love it when something is brand new? The smell of a new car, when you get a new house. Well, one day we will have a new earth! Brides and grooms always look forward to their brand-new life together (those of you who have been married over 20 years know that there are challenges they have no idea will come their way).

Jesus tells us in Revelations 21:5 that. "I am making everything new!" One day everything will be made NEW, a new Heaven, and a new Earth. I am excited to know that I am a part of that as you are. It's the promise of our baptism. Yes, we may have to endure suffering in this life, pain, and loss, but we count on the fact that our home in Heaven is going to be BRAND NEW and that there will be no more pain and suffering, no more tears and anguish.

Today is a BRAND-NEW day, and it's going to be exactly what you make out of it. So, celebrate the gift of something NEW and look around at all of the blessings you have.

Today is going to be a great BRAND-NEW blessed day!

July 6

As I sit and have my cup of coffee with Jesus, I was reflecting on the phrase "God alone suffices." What wisdom we can gain from the Saints. As the sun is rising, I look out and see a beautiful day on the horizon. So what do we have to fear?

Sometimes we have to make an effort to remove the negativity in our thinking and just bask in the presence of the Almighty. Today reminds me of when I was a child. We would ride our bikes in the neighborhood as long as we were home before the streetlights came on. We might go to the park, or swim at someone's house, but there was always time to enjoy the day and each other. Today everybody is busy, everyone is in a hurry. I would love to remind you what busy stands for:

B- Being
U- Under
S- Satan's
Y- Yolk

So today, don't get too busy. Make time for people. Put a smile on your face and have a wonderful day!

July 7

As I sit and have my cup of coffee with Jesus, I was thinking about the NEWS. I used to love to watch the NEWS faithfully, but over the past few years, I don't watch it anymore. I feel it's all BAD NEWS. I really don't know who to believe or if they are even reporting the truth.

That is why I substituted my time watching the NEWS with reading the GOOD NEWS. If you want to find peace and balance in your life, it's necessary to get to know Christ. One of the best ways to do that is to read his WORD, the GOOD NEWS. The scriptures are better at helping us through our problems than anything else.

So today, instead of turning on the television, or reading the newspaper, pick up your Bible and read the GOOD NEWS. I'll give you a hint. It's about love, joy, forgiveness, and peace! That should whet your appetite.

Have a blessed day!

July 8

As I sit and have my cup of coffee with Jesus, I am thinking about the word BALANCE. It's not always easy to keep our spiritual, emotional, psychological, and physical life in BALANCE. Yesterday during my workout, my trainer talked to us about BALANCE, so necessary especially the older we get. She had us do all kinds of exercises to help us keep balanced.

I think the most difficult area for me to stay balanced is physically. If my workout partners did not come every day, I would be out getting a doughnut somewhere. But because they're just so diligent, they help me to find that balance. I think it's important to find people who can keep you accountable in the area in which you find it the most difficult to stay balanced.

Jesus wants us to live a BALANCED life! Thank you, Diana, Tonia, Greg, and Mikey, for keeping me balanced. I think we are in about year 15 with a routine. Even though I'm not excited when I see my trainer show up, (I want doughnut!), I know this routine keeps me balanced. Today, find someone to take a walk with, to go for a run with, to ride a bike with, and find that physical BALANCE.

Have a great day!

July 9

As I sit and have my cup of coffee with Jesus, I was reflecting on how much we RUSH and how much NOISE we create. So I came up with the phrase, "Not the RUSH, but the HUSH." It is important for our souls that we slow down and take moments of quiet. Sometimes we fill our time with noise. Psalm 46:10 says, "Be still and know that I am God." And Psalm 62:5 says, "For God alone, oh my soul, wait in silence, for my hope is from HIM."

Sometimes we need to quiet ourselves down so that we can hear HIS voice. That will take away the rush and busyness of the day and calm our hearts.

So today, on this beautiful morning, don't RUSH, but HUSH, and listen to the sound of HIS voice as HE leads you through the day!

Have a blessed, noise-free day.

July 10

As I sit and have my cup of coffee with Jesus, I was reflecting on 2 Corinthians 12:10. One of the translations says, "Therefore, I take pleasure in being without strength, being insulted, experiencing emergencies, and being chased and forced into a corner for Christ's sake; for when I am without strength, I am DYNAMIC."

So many people I speak with are going through difficult times, yet they are amazing, DYNAMIC people. When I hear stories of what people endure and yet claim Christ for their strength, I am inspired. They may be sorting through things or trying to make sense of the pain they carry, but what I really see is their witness of the love of God in them. These are true heroes of faith.

Today I am going to pray specifically for those who are going through difficult times, that they may continue to be witnesses of faith. These are the people that are DYNAMIC and inspirational, not because everything is easy for them, but that Christ lives through them and their suffering! Thank you for your witness. You know who you are, and you inspire me!

Have a blessed, dynamic day!

July 11

As I sit and have my cup of coffee with Jesus, I was thinking about PROBLEM-SOLVING. I know a lot of friends who were raised to not talk about their problems, and that denial has caused them even greater issues. Sometimes we spend more time reacting to a problem than just taking care of it, just solving it.

All people have problems they have to work through. Just because you have problems does not mean that God is punishing you; in fact, that is absurd. Problems are just a part of life, but what we do with them is the real test. We need to focus to solve them. Sometimes this means setting aside time in the morning to work on them. When we face our problems, it is easy to stay focused in the present moment.

So today, face and SOLVE only today's problems. Don't worry about yesterday's; there is nothing you can do about them. Turn to God and ask for guidance and help! For it says in Philippians 4:6, "Do not be anxious about anything, but in everything by prayer and supplication, with thanksgiving let your request be made known to God." And Proverbs 3:5 says, "Trust in the Lord with all your heart. I do not lean on your own understanding." And Matthew 7:7 says, "Ask, and it will be given to you; seek, and you will find it; knock, and it will be open to you."

Today, turn to the Lord, solve the problems at hand, and then let them go to live in HIS peace and love!

Have a great day!

July 12

Today as I have my cup of coffee (and scone) with Jesus, I was thinking about *blessings*! From simple blessings, like how glad I am that it's a nice day and that the sun is shining or that the grandkids are coming over. I feel blessed that I have wonderful friends. I feel blessed that Jesus has stayed close and has spoken to me in so many ways. I feel blessed each morning to sit out here on my porch and watch this wonderful world wake up and bring *hope*. Even the heat can be a blessing.

We are here, blessed that we had an opportunity to slow down, to simplify, to sanctify, and to focus on what's important. We need to focus on the blessings that God has carried us through rough times and know that He will take us through the rest.

When you feel blessed, it's hard to complain. When you feel blessed, it's hard to be negative. When you feel blessed, you feel alive!

Thank you, Lord, for all of the blessings that you have given me, are giving me, and will give me.

Have a blessed day.

July 13

As I sit and have my cup of coffee with Jesus, I was reflecting on the word TRANSITION. If you look it up in the dictionary, the word is defined as the process or period of change from one state of condition to another. We all go through transitions in our lives. Maybe you have been through a divorce, or a job change, or moved to a new area, or lost someone you love; all of these bring us to TRANSITION.

We cannot stop TRANSITION from happening, but we can certainly rely on Christ to help us through. It says in Joshua 1:9, "Be strong and courageous. Do not be frightened, and do not be dismayed, for the Lord your God is with you wherever you go!" And Jeremiah 29:11 says, "For I know the plans I have for you, declares the Lord, plans for welfare and not for evil, to give you a future full of hope." The scriptures are full of reminders that when we are in TRANSITION, we need to lean on the Lord.

So today, I am going to see the TRANSITIONS in my life as true blessings and a gift from God. I will cling to HIM for direction and support.

Have a great and blessed day!

July 14

As I sit and have my cup of coffee with Jesus, I was thinking of a quote by Samuel Rutherford. He says," The secret formula of the saints is: When I am in the cellar of AFFLICTION, I look for the Lord's choicest wines."

This quote caught my eye on many levels. First, I like wine. And secondly, not only have I had the personal experience of being in the cellar of affliction, but I have also been blessed over the years with people sharing stories of their own afflictions with me. Whether it be the loss of a loved one, a struggle with an addiction, or the fear of living in anxiety or depression, at one time or another we have all known what it is like to enter into the cellar of AFFLICTION. The key is to taste the choicest wines. In our pain, hold onto the only thing that leads us through our affliction, the BLOOD OF CHRIST!

Today, look at how Jesus has carried you through afflictions in your own life. He has never abandoned you or left you alone. Rather, He invites you to drink from the cup! So hold it with two hands and taste the choicest wine!

Have a blessed day!

July 15

As I sit and have my cup of coffee with Jesus, I was thinking of the word CHANGE. As much as we don't always like it, everything is CHANGING. Even time changes every day. When we try to hold onto things too tightly, we struggle with CHANGE.

Jesus teaches us to live in the moment, and to allow change to happen because HE has a plan. The scriptures tell us in 2 Corinthians 5:17, "Therefore, if anyone is in Christ, the new creation has come: the old has gone, the new is here!" And Isaiah 43:19 says, "See, I am doing a new thing! Now it springs up; do you not perceive it? I am making a way in the wilderness and streams in the wasteland."

Today, embrace change, give praise to God for the changes that are happening in your life, and in your family, and in your community, and in our world. Don't be afraid of change. Know that it all is a gift From God!

And have a blessed day.

July 16

As I am having my cup of coffee this morning with Jesus, a father on his bike was being followed by his five-year-old son on his bike with training wheels. I thought about how the FATHER leads us. HE gives us training "wills"! HE teaches us gradually how to surrender our will to HIS! We spend so much of our time working for titles, a bigger house, more money, and our egos can grow strong. We lose our focus and purpose, and then God steps in and teaches us to surrender. We do not have to be afraid because HE is always WITH US, training us, reminding us, picking us up, and loving us.

We all need training! Today let's ask ourselves what is HE training me for? Am I listening, am I following, am I surrendering? Am I following HIM to lead me like that little kid on his bike with training wheels, following his father? Another day for us to grow in HIS awareness and follow HIM.

Here they come, back again. How ironic that this time the little boy is leading.

July 17

As I sit outside having my coffee with Jesus, I was thinking about a phrase that I came across yesterday, "Stand firm." I found it in 1Corinthians16:13; "Be watchful, stand firm in faith, be strong. And Ephesians 6:11 says, "Put on the whole armor of God that you may be able to stand firm against the schemes of the devil. And in 1 Peter:5, "Resist him, stand firm in your faith, knowing that the same kinds of suffering are being experienced by others throughout the world."

Sometimes it's easy to want to throw in the towel or to give up the fight. Sometimes we begin to lose our patience or become negative and critical. It is certainly easy in times when the norm is not the norm.

But we can gain strength from the words of Christ to stand firm. Stand firm that this too shall pass. Stand firm so that we can make a difference. Stand firm that we can grow and become better people. Stand firm in the word and presence of Jesus, even in the storm.

Today, let us stand firm in our belief that all is in the hands of Jesus. HE can lead us through any trial to a deeper relationship with HIM. What a wonderful day for us to stand firm and know that, with Christ, we will conquer.

Have a blessed day!

July 18

As I sit and have my cup of coffee with Jesus, I was thinking about the word PATIENCE. Philippians 4:6 says, "Do not be anxious about anything but in every situation, by prayer and petition, with thanksgiving, present your requests to God."

Some days I find myself impatient with many things. I might be impatient with my children, or my grandchildren, or with people who come to see me, or with the dog, or with my calendar, and the list goes on and on. I'm trying to practice the art of pausing before I act or respond. During this pause, I take a breath and try to be conscious of what is actually going on.

So today, I am going to practice the art of being PATIENT, not only with others but with myself. I'm going to try to be mindful of taking that pause, mindful that I need to stay present in the moment so that I can respond with love and care.

Today, let us practice the art of being PATIENT and celebrate our Lord, who is very PATIENT with us.

Have a blessed day!

July 19

As I sit and have my cup of coffee with Jesus, I am thinking about the word STRENGTH. A friend of mine sent me a reflection by Danielle Koepke. She says, "Being strong means refusing to tolerate people and things that wound your soul." It is not always easy to be STRONG. A good question to ask ourselves is what are we afraid of? Where can I get strength from?

Scriptures remind us of where our strength comes from. Strength comes from within. Nehemiah 8:10 says, "Do not grieve, for the joy of the Lord is your strength." And Isaiah 41:10 says, "So do not fear, for I am with you; do not be dismayed for I am your God. I will STRENGTHEN you and help you; I will uphold you with my righteous right hand." Remember the story of David and Goliath? God gave David the strength to face a giant!

Strength comes when we are centered in Christ, when we are not afraid of anything, because we know HE leads us. We gain strength so that each day we can set out to do GOD'S WILL! When we allow the GOD that lives within us to guide our feet, we are strong! When we are afraid, we lack trust in the promises of Christ.

So today, greet the day with the strength of the God that lives within you. Put a smile on your face, make a difference in the world, and shine. There's nothing to be afraid of when our strength comes from God.

Have a blessed day!

July 20

As I sit and have my cup of coffee with Jesus, I was thinking about WORKING OUT. I seem to be very disciplined in my prayer life, and I like routine, but working out takes a lot of effort for me. I know I should do it, I feel better once I've done it, and I know it's good for my body, so why do I struggle? I know all this, and yet, as I sit here having my cup of coffee with Jesus, all I can think about are all the ways I can get out of my WORKOUT this morning. Pancakes and scones sound so much better!

Today, however, I am going to listen to my inner voice that tells me I need this in more ways than one. I know it will help me in the ministry GOD calls me to today, and it will help me to think more clearly and to feel good. I am going to make it part of my prayer today to exercise.

So today, join me. Get out and take care of your body. Take a walk, go on a hike, go to the gym, do something to continue to celebrate health and God's call to take care of the temple of the Holy Spirit. I'm heading into the gym right now, but maybe I'll go for pancakes after my workout!

Have a blessed day!

July 21

As I sit and have my cup of coffee with Jesus, I was thinking about the word *anticipation*. Think about all the times you really get excited about something and the anticipation that builds up. I get really excited when I hear my grandkids are coming to visit. I try to get some fun things planned and try to cancel other things so that I can be truly present. And the anticipation grows and grows until they get here.

With all of the changes that have taken place in my life, I am working hard to be excited about all of these simple moments, because building relationships and sharing love is more important than all the work you can do. I am working very hard at trying to be present in the moment and present to the people I'm with. I'm working hard on being grateful for all the blessings that God has given me and the way he continues to show me His presence in my journey.

Today, get excited! Anticipate surprises and know that God loves you.

And have a blessed day.

July 22

As I sit and have my cup of coffee with Jesus, I am continuing my reflection on *anger*. Anger is a real emotion; we should not deny it. But we have to be very careful with it. We cannot ignore anger. Rather, we need to be careful when we allow it to control us.

I have read some great quotes on anger. One said, "Anger doesn't solve anything, it builds nothing, but he can destroy everything." Another one said, "Speak when you are angry, and you'll make the best speech you'll never forget!" Ralph Waldo Emerson said, "For every minute you remain angry, you give up sixty-seconds of peace of mind." Aristotle said, "Anyone can become angry—that is easy, but to be angry with the right person and to the right degree and at the right time and for the right purpose, and in the right way—that is not within everybody's power and is not easy." Even Jesus got angry. You remember the story when He overturned the tables in the temple.

When we take our *anger* to prayer, God can help us to soften the blow or help us to regroup to breathe his grace into the moment. Today, lift up your *anger*. Learn to calm yourself, give space and time to whoever or whatever angers you, and allow God in! Don't waste another minute!

Have a blessed day…

July 23

As I sit and have my cup of coffee with Jesus, I was thinking about the expression "to gaze." To gaze is to go out of self. Joni Eareckson Tada says, "I want to stay in the habit of 'glancing' at my problems and 'gazing' at the Lord." That is something that I, too, want to learn to do.

Yesterday, a young couple stopped by to introduce me to their new baby. To watch the way in which they gazed at their child was amazing. What a wonderful day it can be when we gaze upon the Lord and all of His wonderment, instead of being distracted by drama, violence, and fear.

Today, on this beautiful morning, *gaze* on the Lord with joy, amazement, and gratitude! It is a beautiful day when you *gaze* upon the love of the Father, Son, and Holy Spirit.

Have a wonderful day!

July 24

As I sit and have my cup of coffee with Jesus, I was thinking about this NEW day. There are some things I need to get done today. I have a number of appointments and some people I need to check on, but I really want to be PRESENT AND POSITIVE. I want to be PRESENT in my attitude, my speech, and my awareness throughout the day. I want to acknowledge all of God's blessings as they take place.

It's easy to become overwhelmed with what we have planned for the day, but it's even more amazing when we change our ATTITUDE and awaken. As the sun rises this morning, I see God's creation coming alive. Today, I'm going to work on my attitude, praising GOD while unloading the dishwasher, or meeting with friends, or reading and writing.

Today, pour yourself a cup of coffee, and take a few moments to make this the best day. For this is the day the Lord has made. Let us rejoice and be glad in it. It is a wonderful world!

Have a blessed day.

July 25

As I sit and have my cup of coffee with Jesus, I was thinking about SELF TRUST. It's hard, sometimes, to TRUST ourselves, but it is also the core of our existence. If we believe that Christ lives in us, then TRUSTING ourselves is very important. Both doubt and fear are our enemies. Anxiety, confusion, and depression is against the very spirit of God that lives in us. We learn SELF TRUST by listening, by making mistakes and by TRUSTING ourselves anyway.

We learn SELF TRUST by listening to God, who lives within us. In reality, we know what is best for us, and we also know what takes us down. We have to learn to TRUST ourselves! We can look to others for support and help, but we have to TRUST ourselves. When we stand in our own TRUST, and in our own light, Christ lives in us. 11 Philippians 4:13 says, "I can do all things through him who strengthens me." And Psalm 28:7 says, "The Lord is my strength and my shield; and in Him my heart TRUSTS; and I am helped, my heart exults, and with my song I will give thanks to him."

Today listen to your inner voice that is the Christ who lives within you, who guides you. Trust in yourself, and say the beautiful prayer of the DIVINE MERCY, "Jesus I TRUST in you!"

Have a blessed day!

July 26

As I sit and have my cup of coffee with Jesus, I was thinking about the power of LISTENING. Being able to LISTEN to others, to creation, and especially to God, takes effort. It's easy to talk, or try to make your point, and for some, it's easy to argue. But to really take time to listen to what someone else has to say is an art.

Have you ever sat outside and listened to the birds sing, or the crashing of the ocean waves, or even to majestic silence? When we LISTEN, we slow our brains down and take away the noise from the world. It's easy to pray by rambling off words, or repeating prayers, but the gift of prayer is LISTENING to the voice of God as He speaks to our hearts!

Today, on this beautiful morning as the sun prepares to come up, I'm going to say the prayers and read the reflections I do every day. But today, I'm going to make an effort to LISTEN to God tell me of the GLORIOUS things He has planned for me. I am sure that HIS list of things for me to do that is far greater and life-giving than the one I have prepared!

Have a blessed day…and LISTEN!

July 27

As I sit and have my cup of coffee with Jesus, I was thinking of a phrase that Jesus said in Mark 4:39, "PEACE, BE STILL." Sometimes people think that self-talk is not good. I think it is essential! Everybody thinks too much and about too many things. When we're thinking all the time, it's hard to live in the present moment, and the words, "PEACE, BE STILL" need to be repeated. Just as Jesus calmed the wind and the sea with the words, "PEACE, BE STILL," HE does the same with the worry, anxiety, and frustration we experience.

When we are STILL, our senses are stronger. We become more aware of the sounds of creation, the smells and the sights of miracles unfolding every moment. Saint Francis of Assisi learned this in his lifetime. It allowed him to experience God in the city, in the mountains, in creation, wherever life took him.

Today, repeat those words often as you go about your day. Speak to yourself the healing words of Christ," PEACE, BE STILL."

And have a blessed day!

July 28

As I sit and have my cup of coffee with Jesus, I was thinking about the word *inspire*. I reflect on how God's Word inspires me to move forward each day with a positive attitude. And I think of all the people who have inspired me over the years. I think about my parents, the wonderful teachers and coaches I had in school, the priests and ministers who have been an inspiration to me. Many of them have been through trials themselves and still kept their heads up high. They have inspired me to want to better know Jesus.

Today, I am going to name these special people in my heart and thank God for those who remind me that Jesus is Lord. And that with His Spirit, we, too, can inspire others. Welcome to *inspiration*.

Have a great day. Put on a smile and be inspirational!

July 29

It's a beautiful morning, having my cup of coffee with Jesus. I watch the sun come up, and I'm really thinking and praying about a *new* day. I have some things that I want to get done and some people to check on and talk to, but I also want to be present in my attitude and my speech throughout the day.

I want to notice all of the blessings God places before me today. A neighbor is walking by with his dog and says good morning to me. That might be a common phrase, but today, it feels fresh and new. It is a good morning. It becomes a good day when I change my attitude, when I see the endless things that can happen which have allowed me to experience God. As the sun rises, I see God's creation coming alive, the birds are singing, and everything is green. And I praise God.

I do have things to do today, but it's all about my attitude. I'm asking God to give me an attitude of gratitude all day. From unloading the dishwasher, tutoring grandchildren, listening to people share their stories, and being present in the moment, it's all about attitude, and we need to begin first thing in the morning.

So pour yourself a cup of coffee. Take a few moments to reflect on the fact that this is the day the Lord has made. Let us rejoice and be glad in it.

July 30

As I sit and have my cup of coffee with Jesus, I was thinking about the word *foundation*. Foundations are very important. For some, we had parents who laid a very strong and healthy foundation. For others, they had to build their own. Maybe they have been blessed to have had teachers, coaches, mentors, or spiritual leaders who helped them build a strong foundation.

Today is a great day to reflect on who helped you build your foundation Who helped you get to where you are today? As Christians, we are blessed that Jesus has become our foundation. It's by His Word that we build our lives. Our faith in Him has become the cornerstone in which we base our lives today. It doesn't matter whether you started with a weak foundation or a strong one, what matters is that Christ is the cornerstone of that foundation, and not even Satan can touch that!

Have a beautiful day and take some time today to reflect on the foundation that holds you up!

July 31

As I sit and have my cup of coffee with Jesus, I was thinking about *laughter*. I think it's so important that we laugh. I think that laughter is healing. It's good to laugh. We have to learn not to take life so seriously.

Oftentimes, my grandchildren are the best forms of laughter. My grandson was here for a few hours, and I asked him how old he thought I was. He said seventy-eight! When I told him I am only sixty-one, we just sat and laughed.

Today, laugh! Laugh at yourself and then find someone to laugh with. There's a lot of serious things going on in the world, but we have to remember that everything is in Jesus's hands, so it's going to be okay.

Have a blessed day, and remember, it's even okay to laugh at yourself!

August 1

As I sit and have my cup of coffee with Jesus, I was thinking about SELF-AWARENESS. The Bible tells us in 1 Timothy 4:16, "Keep a close watch on yourself and on the teaching. Persist in this, for by doing so you will save both yourself and your hearers."

It is important for us to have self-awareness. In 2 Corinthians 13:5 it says, "Examine yourselves, to see whether you are in the faith. Test yourselves. Or do you not realize this about yourselves, that Jesus Christ is in you?" Every day when we wake up and when we go to bed, we should do some self-reflection. We should examine ourselves and be aware of how our day has gone, or how we can be better, or whether we responded like Christ. True self-awareness helps us to see the Christ that lives in us.

Today, take time to reflect and be aware of yourself and the Christ that lives within you. When you do, you become a light in a world where there is a lot of darkness. We need the light more than ever.

Have a blessed day and be aware of the great GIFT you are!

August 2

As I sit and have my cup of coffee with Jesus, I was thinking about a phrase I came across yesterday, "STAND FIRM." I found it in 1 Corinthians 16:13, "Be watchful, STAND FIRM in faith, be strong." Ephesians 6:11 says, "Put on the whole armor of God that you may be able to STAND FIRM against the schemes of the devil." And in 1 Peter 5 it says, "Resist him, STAND FIRM in your faith, knowing that the same kinds of suffering are being experienced by others throughout the world."

Sometimes it is easy to want to throw in the towel or to give up the fight. We can sometimes begin to lose our patience or become negative or critical. It is certainly easy these days when the norm no longer seems to be the norm. So we can gain strength from the words of Christ, "STAND FIRM." Stand firm, that this too will pass. STAND FIRM, that we can make a difference. STAND FIRM, that we can grow and become better people. STAND FIRM in the WORD and presence of Jesus, even in the storm.

Today, let us STAND FIRM in our belief that all is in the hands of Jesus. Jesus walks with us through our trials. And these trials will bring us into a deeper relationship with HIM.

STAND FIRM and smile! And have a blessed day.

August 3

As I sit and have my cup of coffee with Jesus, I was thinking about a book I read years ago called, "Don't Sweat the Small Stuff." I know this saying is true, but it's harder to practice living it. It makes me wonder why I make such a long To Do List every day, or why I have trouble sitting still and reflecting, or how I get annoyed when something I plan doesn't go just the way I wanted.

When we choose to follow Jesus, we can't "sweat the small stuff." Jesus is always bringing us sacred interruptions to see if we can find the HOLINESS in the moment. We can learn that we do not have to control the moment; rather, we can actually be present in it. Whether it be a house that needs to be cleaned, or a flat tire, or the endless list, our attitude makes all the difference. Are we serving our To Do list or our Lord? Can we see the lessons in the sacred interruptions? Are we holding onto the past or embracing the present? When we strive to put Jesus in the center of our lives, it's all small stuff!

Today, I will strive to see Jesus in all the simple tasks, the small things, and make them prayers of GRATITUDE. I think I will put that on my list!

Have a blessed day.

August 4

As I sit and have my cup of coffee with Jesus, I was thinking about the power of POSITIVE THINKING. It is so easy to look around and complain, to feel that everything is going wrong. But, as Christians, we are called to see God's hand in everything.

Maybe you've spent a lifetime around negative people and have absorbed that disease. Negative thinking empowers the problem. We need to find the balance in our lives and open our eyes to what is good each and every day. We need to bring the POSITIVE message of the GOSPEL. Positive energy heals, brings love, and transforms!

The scriptures remind us in Philippians 4:8, "Finally, brothers and sisters, whatever is true, whatever is honorable, whatever is just, whatever is pure, whatever is lovely, whatever is commendable, if there is any excellence, if there is anything worthy of praise, think about these things."

Today, make it a POSITIVE day. Fill the morning with positive thoughts. Bring the POSITIVE message of Christ to the world.

Have a blessed day!

August 5

As I sit and have my cup of coffee with Jesus, I think of the word NEIGHBOR. I am blessed to live in a wonderful neighborhood. I don't think a day goes by that I don't see someone doing something kind for someone else. Yesterday, I sat on my porch on a beautiful afternoon and saw a NEIGHBOR across the street take some food to another NEIGHBOR who has been under the weather. I watched some families ride by on their bikes; they stopped to say hello. And there were lots of dog walkers and people out planting flowers in their gardens, taking time to chat.

It's important to get to know your NEIGHBORS. So much fear has come into our world that people are afraid to get to know each other. Neighborhoods are really just small communities, but together we can do great things.

So, today I am going to pray for my NEIGHBORHOOD and see what I can do to be a better NEIGHBOR. Today, be a great NEIGHBOR, get to know the people around you, and try to build a community based on peace and love. Jesus would expect nothing less.

Have a blessed day, Neighbor!

August 6

As I sit and have my cup of coffee with Jesus, I was thinking about the word PERSPECTIVE. No matter how wonderful life seems to be going, if our spirit is crushed, it's almost impossible for us to experience joy! But when our PERSPECTIVE is Heaven, we can endure almost anything!

Fifty years from now, most of us will be long gone and everything we went through on this earth will have no more meaning. The only thing that will matter is eternal life. The scriptures tell us in Romans 8:18, "I consider that the sufferings of the present time are not worth comparing with the glory that is to be revealed to us." Everything we go through, everything that God allows us to experience, is preparing us for eternal life in HIS presence!

So today, realize all of the suffering, pain, and loss is nothing compared to the promise of eternal life, where there will be no more suffering, tears, or pain. Keep things in PERSPECTIVE and know that today is going to be an amazing day, one day closer to being with the KING of KINGS.

Have a blessed day!

August 7

As I sit and have my cup of coffee with Jesus, I was reflecting on INNER STILLNESS. Two years ago, I went through a personal crisis. During that time, I was paralyzed, overwhelmed by circumstances, filled with intense anxiety and helplessness. Even thinking about it now brings tension into my body. Inside my heart, I could hear only a whisper, "Be still and know that I AM GOD." Something greater than me and my circumstances was holding me together.

Even today, I seek that stillness, that moment where I can find the truth that God is WITH me. Don't get me wrong…it's been a long journey, but the voice gets louder, and as I become more still, the only thing I hear are the words, "Be still, and know that I am God."

Today, as I begin my day, I take a moment to be STILL and listen to that voice that speaks from my inner soul. I continue to forgive, and I know that will bring me to the peace that only comes from HIM! Find that Stillness and you will find HIS PEACE!

Have a blessed day. And remember these words, "Be still and know that I am God."

August 8

As I sit and have my cup of coffee with Jesus (with my new mug!), I am thinking about the need to REACH OUT. Sometimes in our daily walk, our energy is low. We might be fighting depression or we just feel overwhelmed with problems. That is when we should hear the words from our Lord, "REACH OUT!"

In times like that, we need to go outside ourselves and reach out to others. Call a friend, visit someone who is sick, write a card to somebody who is in the hospital, make sandwiches for the homeless; do something to get out of self. REACH OUT!

And while you are reaching out, REACH OUT to the Lord. Ask HIM to bring light into your life and into your heart. Ask HIM to inspire you so that you can inspire others. Ask HIM to lift you out of darkness into his loving embrace.

REACH OUT, and have a blessed day.

August 9

As I sit and have my cup of coffee with Jesus, I was thinking about how important it is to have a positive attitude in PRAYER. Sometimes PRAYER can be rather routine, like marking something off of the To-Do list. But sometimes PRAYER can be deep and contemplative.

What I have come to realize is that it is my attitude that is what is important. When I pray, I bring myself present to the Lord and allow my SOUL to reach out to touch MY CREATOR. When I have a POSITIVE attitude, my PRAYER is that much more powerful. I find myself full of gratitude and blessings. The problems have not gone away. There is still a long list of things to do, but, for that moment, I allow my soul to touch HIM. With open arms, HE embraces me and lets me know that everything is going to be OK; actually, not just OK, but WONDERFUL.

Today, take a moment to PRAY! PRAY with thanksgiving and praise. PRAY with confidence and trust. And then let me know what happens, because there's nothing like hearing someone share their story of meeting God face-to-face.

Have a blessed day!

August 10

As I sit and have my cup of coffee with Jesus, I was reflecting on a book I reread this week called *The Wounded Healer* by Henri Nouwen. It made me think about all of the woundedness in this world, of all the broken lives. I think of my own life and how I have experienced such darkness and brokenness.

To be broken may be painful, but I know I was not alone. Jesus was close to me through it all. I believe it was part of the bigger plan. Jesus allows us to go through difficult things so that we can be dependent on the Father. When we go through tough times, are attacked, or feel abandoned, we have to put our trust in Him.

Today, I pray that my wounds may help others heal, and that together, our wounds will make up the body of Christ.

Have a blessed day.

August 11

As I sit and have my cup of coffee with Jesus, I was thinking about the word *patience*. The definition of *patience* is the capacity to accept trouble or suffering without getting angry or upset. It's not easy to be *patient* with one another. I often pray that God gives me *patience* when things don't go exactly as I planned, when I get "sacred interruptions." These are interruptions that I don't plan but that God puts in front of me just to see how I will do.

In Romans 12:12, it says, "Rejoice in *hope*, be *patient* in tribulation, be constant in prayer." And Ephesians 4:2 says, "With all humility and gentleness, with *patience*, bearing with one another in love." As Christians, to practice the art of *patience* is a great goal for us. Whether we are in line waiting for something, frustrated that things are not running smoothly, or are unable to find understanding from others, in *prayer*, we can practice the art of *patience*.

Today, I am going to not only be patient with others but with myself. Try it and have a blessed day!

August 12

As I sit and have my cup of coffee with Jesus, I was thinking about the word AWARE. Yesterday, I sat on my porch for a little bit and threw the ball to my dog, Francis. I started looking around and I became AWARE of so many things. I noticed that the trees were in full bloom. There were a lot of tangerines on my neighbor's tree and, I must confess, they were very sweet. I watched neighbors walk by, waving or stopping to say hello, others in a hurry as they rushed through the streets.

Awareness is something I need to practice more often. A hummingbird just came, and I sat so still that it just stayed right in front of me. It made me think of all the times I have missed seeing God's presence because I was in such a hurry or too much in my own mind. I didn't see all of God's miracles happening right before my very eyes.

So today, I am going to practice AWARENESS. Awareness in the simple things, in the sound of the birds, in the colors in the sunset, in cloud formations, and in all of the other gifts that God has in store for me today!

Have a blessed day and try to be aware of all that God brings your way.

August 13

As I sit and have my cup of coffee with Jesus, I noticed that a lot of people have been sending me messages about *forgiveness*. I believe forgiveness needs to happen every day, at every moment. I made a list of people I know I need to forgive. It was really not that long, but doing it was a very painful exercise. I pray every day that I will release that pain and hurt so that I can truly live the *gospel*.

Jesus says to forgive seventy times seven. Don't wait to forgive people, because you may lose the opportunity to forgive or to be forgiven. Do not hold on to hurt and pain. Ask not only to be given the grace to forgive others, but also the grace to forgive ourselves for holding on to pain.

So today, make a list of those people you need to forgive and ask for God's grace. Don't wait one more moment! Jesus never waited to forgive! God is waiting for us to follow the *gospel*!

Have a blessed day!

August 14

As I sit and have my cup of coffee with Jesus, I was reflecting on the word *ego*. You can tell when ego runs a person's life. They feel very important, and yet you can see their lack of *joy* and *authenticity*. Oftentimes, they use their egos to threaten and beat down others in order to look better themselves. When the *ego* takes over, watch out, because Jesus and ego do not go together.

We also need to be careful that we do not get caught up in other people's egos. Those with strong egos, also known as narcissists, will continue to bully, lie, and do whatever they need to feed those egos. The best thing to do is to pray for them and keep your own ego in check.

Jesus says we must die to self; that is, to our *ego*. Sometimes, it is good to make a change in our lives to get out of the ego control. Today is a great day to look at ourselves, to look at our own egos, and look at the egos that try to take us down. Stay close to the Lord, and you won't have to worry about them doing anything to you; they will only destroy themselves.

Have a blessed day, and keep that ego in check!

August 15

As I sit and have my cup of coffee with Jesus, I was thinking about *self-peace*. Francis, my dog, and I decided to escape to the beach where we ran into friends, and we began talking about *self-peace*. There's a difference between the *peace* we sometimes feel in the world and *self-peace*. Self-peace comes from the inside, knowing that we are living God's plan in our lives and content even with chaos, attacks, and pain.

Self-peace requires a deep relationship with Christ, trusting that He will carry us through life. And there is even purpose in the trials that we go through. When we find *self-peace*, we find the presence of God.

Today, I'm going to strive for *self-peace*, a peace that draws me into the sacredness of the relationship of the Father, Son, and Spirit. What a gift *self-peace* is!

Have a blessed day.

August 16

As I sit and have my cup of coffee with Jesus, I was thinking of the word *waiting*. We might be waiting for a relationship to change, waiting for good news, or waiting for a doctor's report. We might be waiting for a loved one to return home or waiting for a package to come.

When God brings us a time of *waiting*, it sometimes seems like He is nonresponsive. We get anxious, and we try to fill that time of waiting with other things without realizing the waiting might really be God's way of sanctification. We need to wait for God's timing because it is perfect; it will not disappoint us. We need to wait for God to *move* in His own time.

So today, I'm going to *patiently* wait. I am going to trust that God has a reason for everything under the sun. And while I wait, I will continue to know, love, and serve Him! Psalm 27:14 says, "Wait for the Lord; be strong and take heart and wait for the Lord!"

Have a blessed day.

August 17

As I sit and have my cup of coffee with Jesus, I was thinking about how I sometimes feel like just a tiny drop of water in the ocean. When I get caught up in the negativity of so many people's different ideologies and movements, some of them so mean-spirited, I get frustrated. I feel like I'm swimming upstream.

But then, I hear the voice of God, who calls me to silence. He teaches me to swim with the current of His grace. Don't get me wrong. There are times when we also have to swim upstream against the current to do what is right, trusting that God will give us the courage and the strength.

Today, I am going to go with the flow and let God take me where He needs to take me, knowing that He guides me and directs me! He teaches me to swim to a new place, ready to set foot on an island of truth and *hope*. God is my compass.

I am remembering my father today on his birthday!

Have a blessed day.

August 18

As I sit and have my cup of coffee with Jesus, I was thinking about the word *focus*. One of my grandchildren was telling me how hard it was for him to *focus*. Then a friend of mine called and also said he had a hard time focusing, how his mind kept wandering when he was reading the scriptures, trying to pray. At times, I think that all of us have some kind of fog that keeps us from being able to *focus*. We may be struggling with focusing on even some of the simplest things. Last night, I went downstairs and I couldn't remember why I went down there. And I still don't!

But I do know that what I am going to focus on today: God's love. Every day that we wake up, God breathes new life into us. We don't need to overthink it, we don't really even have to focus on it, we just have to gratefully accept it.

So today, don't worry if you can't remember what you're doing or even why you're doing it. Just remember God loves you, and when you're confused, think of Him!

And have a blessed day!

August 19

As I sit and have my cup of coffee with Jesus, I was thinking about the gift of *friendship*. You come to know who your real friends are when you go through tough times in life. I thought about the kind of friend I am. Do I reach out to people when they are suffering, sick, or troubled? Am I a true friend, or am I just one when it is convenient? And it can be painful when friendships change or end.

True friends are hard to come by, but when we find one, it's like finding a rare pearl. Jesus wants to be our friend, someone we can trust. Jesus is there for us to share our fears and trials, knowing that He will stand by us.

Today, I'm going to pray in a special way for all my friends, even my four-legged ones, and pray that I can be a good friend. And I am going to thank God for the gift of friendships, true friendships. And I am going to reach out to a friend in need today.

Have a blessed day!

August 20

As I sit and have my cup of coffee with Jesus, I was thinking about another one of the fruits of the Holy Spirit, JOY! I think that here is a difference between happiness and JOY. We can be going through very difficult times in our lives and still feel moments of JOY. That is when we experience the JOY that Jesus is our Lord and know that there is nothing to worry about.

I'm reading a book by Henry Nouwen, and in it he states that the greatest gift we can give anyone is our own personal inner JOY, peace, silence, solitude, and well-being. We may want to do things for people, or sometimes feel that we're taking on other people's problems and issues (otherwise known as codependency), but that does not really help them. What people need to experience is the inner peace, JOY, and the positive energy that flows from a person who knows the Lord.

Today, I am going to focus on JOY! Everything may not be perfect in my life, but I do feel God's presence deep within my heart, and that brings JOY. That is the greatest gift I can share today!

Have a blessed, joy-filled day.

August 21

As I sit and have my cup of coffee with Jesus, taking a day to catch up with my thoughts, I was thinking of a special verse in scripture that I call my LIFE VERSE. This scripture, from Jeremiah 29:11, speaks to me. It says, "For I know the PLANS I have for you, declares the Lord, plans to PROSPER you and not to harm you, PLANS to give you HOPE and a future." So, I sit here in GRATITUDE, knowing that God loves me so much that He has a plan for me. Being a person who likes to have control reminds me how much more I need to learn to surrender. My only responsibility is to be OPEN to it.

So today, I sit in gratitude for HIS PLAN. I have been blessed with a beautiful family and wonderful grandkids, good friends, their support and a deep FAITH in CHRIST. I don't know why I sometimes doubt there's a PLAN, for He has never let me down. Today I'm going to trust in HIS PLAN!

Have a blessed day!

August 22

As I sit and have my cup of coffee with Jesus this morning, I was reflecting on the word CHANGE. Everything in the world is in motion, and whether we like it or not, everything is always changing.

It says in Romans 8:6, "The mind governed by the flesh is death, but the mind governed by the Spirit is LIFE and PEACE." And Isaiah 40:31 says, "But those who hope in the Lord will RENEW their strength. They will soar on wings of eagles; they will run and not grow weary; they will walk and not be faint."

When God takes you on a journey where you have to face change, embrace HIS WORD. God does not want us to get too comfortable in this life, for this life is not HIS promise. Jeremiah 29:11 has always been my life verse. It says, "I know the plans I have for you, declares the Lord, plans to prosper you and not to harm you, plans to give you HOPE and a FUTURE." So, when God takes you out of your comfort zone and brings CHANGE into your life, it's for HIS purpose. As difficult as that is; embrace it, celebrate it, and live it.

So today, look and see what God is bringing about in your life through change and DON't be afraid. Get excited, because the best part of your life is about to begin!

Have a blessed day!

August 23

As I sit and have my cup of coffee with Jesus, I was reflecting on a quote from John Henry Jowett that says, "God comforts us not to make us comfortable but to make us comforters." Oftentimes, God allows us to experience difficult moments and takes us to places we do not want to go. He does this so that he can use us. He teaches us to COMFORT others.

Do you wonder why you've had to go through certain trials, suffering, or pain? In time, you will see God needed you to experience these things to carry out HIS plan. HE will bring people and situations to you so that you can be the COMFORTER! You will be able to share your story of suffering and how GOD carried you through. God will use you as a gift to others. God will use you to bring hope in times of despair. And I believe there will become a time when you may even praise God for the trial, for it is HIS Grace that has given you TRUE FAITH!

Today, I will strive to accept GOD'S plan and allow HIM to use me as HE needs! And I thank God for the COMFORTERS in my life!

Have a blessed day.

August 24

As I sit and have my cup of coffee with Jesus, I was thinking about all of the people who have been talking to me about loneliness and depression. Both are very real things. If you are one of the lucky ones who doesn't suffer from these afflictions, know that you still play an important part in the lives of those who do.

Throughout my life, I have dealt with depression. I've had some times of loneliness, but I've never really felt alone. Part of that is because I'm an extrovert and I like being around people. But these are serious issues and the scriptures offer us great help when we are feeling down or alone. One of my favorite scriptures is Deuteronomy 31:8, "The Lord HIMSELF goes before you and will be with you. He will never leave you or forsake you. Do not be afraid; do not be discouraged."

So, if you suffer from depression or loneliness, know you're never alone, for the Lord IS with you! And if you don't suffer from these afflictions, know that a simple phone call, a kind word, or a text can make all the difference to those who do! Never be afraid to reach out to someone!

Have a blessed day!

August 25

As I sit and have my cup of coffee with Jesus, I was reflecting on a quote from St. Augustine. It says, "God is always trying to give good things to us, but our hands are too full to receive them." So the question that we need to ask ourselves is what am I filling my hands with? Am I filling my hands with worry, wringing them daily? Am I filling my hands with busyness? Am I filling my hands with greed, or envy, or anger? Maybe I fill my hands with violence, or disrespect, or idleness. Maybe I close my hands all together and keep out love, and grace, and peace! To receive all that GOD gives us, we need to greet HIM with OPEN hands.

Today, I'm going to let go of all the things I'm holding onto so tightly and OPEN my hands to the Lord! While my hands are open, I will offer HIM praise and thanksgiving for all that HE does for me and for all the blessings HE gives me every day. With open hands, I will sing HIS praises.

Have a blessed day!

August 26

As I sit and have my cup of coffee with Jesus, I was thinking about the word *peace*! It is really an amazing word. We can use it to describe inner peace, peace in the family, or peace in our world. I think that before we can strive for peace in our world, it has to begin in our own hearts. The world sometimes forces us to slow down. If we can take a deep breath and be present in the moment, we can find His *peace*. If we don't look at the past and don't worry about the future, but live in the present, in His presence, we can find peace!

Today, I'm going to be aware of my own breath. I am going to take time to look at the changing season. I'm going to become aware that, even in chaos, I can find peace. Jesus said in John 14:27, "My *peace* I leave you; My peace I give you. I do not give it to you as the world gives. Do not let your hearts be troubled and do not be afraid." If we can find this *peace*, then we can pass it on.

Have a *peace*-filled day! And remember, Jesus is called the Prince of Peace.

August 27

As I sit and have my cup of coffee with Jesus, I was reflecting on a quote from St. Francis de Sales, who says, "Do not look forward to what may happen tomorrow; the same everlasting Father who cares for you today will take care of you tomorrow and every day. Either HE will shield you from suffering, or HE will give you unfailing strength to bear it. Be at peace, then, put aside all anxious thoughts and imaginations and say continually: the Lord is my strength and my shield; my heart has trusted in HIM and I am helped. HE is not only with me but in me and I in HIM."

There is so much more we can learn and so much more PEACE we can achieve if we only LISTEN to the Lord. He will give us all we need for today. So, forget about yesterday and don't fret about tomorrow. Live today THROUGH HIM, WITH HIM, AND IN HIM!

Have a blessed day serving HIM!

August 28

As I sit and have my cup of coffee with Jesus, I was thinking about LIFE. Yesterday, my seven-year-old grandson got a Happy Meal and in it was a miniature version of the game of Life. We played it for a couple of hours and laughed over and over again.

Sometimes we can take LIFE too seriously. Instead of basking in the beauty of God's creation, the little miracles HE shows us each day, we get caught up in the problems of LIFE. To truly live means to have a LIFE.

Every once in a while, I say to someone, "You need to get a LIFE!" But the life that God has planned for us is perfect! Sometimes we need to just surrender and go with the flow. There will always be things that challenge us in this LIFE, but when we allow Jesus in, there is nothing we cannot handle.

Today, I am going to celebrate LIFE, not just my personal LIFE, but the LIFE of my community, the life of my family, and the life of my friends. Today, I will celebrate LIFE, with gratitude and thanksgiving.

Have a blessed day!

August 29

As I sit this beautiful morning and have my cup of coffee with Jesus, I am thinking about STRENGTH. What makes us strong? Usually when something difficult comes our way, a special trial or a great sorrow, something that really reshapes our world, which is when we grow STRONG. When God wants to strengthen us, HE allows us to enter a storm. After the storm, we have to clean up the debris. We look around and then we REBUILD. We do things differently too, so that we will be ready for the next trial. And when we look back, we will see that the trial and separation the storm brought was needed to bring us closer to God. And that has made us STRONGER.

Today, I am grateful for the trials, the storms, those moments when I am afraid, because they have made me stronger in my relationship with Christ. I may be battle-scarred, but I have learned that it's not the TITLES we carry BUT the TESTIMONY that matters.

Have a blessed day, knowing you can handle the storms when Christ is your Lord.

August 30

As I sit and have my cup of coffee with Jesus, I was reflecting on *walking* in faith. It's often hard to know what to believe today. What is real news? What is fake news? It can be hard to tell. But we always have His Good News. What I do know is we need to *walk* in faith and the only news we should trust is the Good News of Jesus Christ.

To *walk* in faith means to *trust* in God's Word and in His promises, His commandments. It means being true to *self* while allowing the Spirit of God to direct our lives. How blessed we are that our Creator fills us with His Spirit to be our guide. If we are sad or depressed, going through a trial, or are struggling, we just need to go to His Word (the Good News) and His promises. We may live in confusing times, but God is never confusing.

So today, open the Good News of Jesus Christ. Listen to the *truth* and follow His guidance. In the end, nothing else matters but to be true to self and true to God! Let our prayer be, "Jesus, I surrender myself to you. You take care of everything!"

Have a blessed day!

August 31

As I sit and have my cup of coffee with Jesus, I was thinking about what it means to LET GO. There are so many things we need to LET GO of! We may need to let go of hurts from the past. We may need to let go of relationships or friendships that are unhealthy. We may need to let go of holding in anger and resentment. The good thing about letting go of things is that it makes room to HOLD ON to things that are truly important.

Think of what you need to let go of. Make a list of four or five things that trouble you. Then make a list of four or five things that you want to embrace. As I was working on my list this morning, I had to stop at four or five, because I probably have fifteen things I need to let go of! It's amazing how this small exercise can put things into perspective.

But today, I'm going to pick just four or five. My list of what I need to hold on to is inspired by Jesus. I need to hold onto HIS love, HIS strength, HIS word, HIS forgiveness, and HIS mercy.

Have a blessed day!

September 1

As I sit and have my cup of coffee with Jesus, I was reading this quote, "Just a simple act of kindness goes a long way." Wouldn't our world be a better place if each one of us did just a couple acts of kindness each day? If we would spend less time complaining, being critical, or being impatient and just did simple acts of kindness, we could transform our world!

Throughout this day, Jesus is going to give you opportunities in which you can choose to do *simple acts of kindness*. It might be letting somebody go in front of you at the grocery store, being patient with your children as they struggle to do their homework, or phoning to check on an elderly neighbor…the list goes on and on.

Today, let's make a difference. Let's see how many simple acts of kindness we can do to bring the *presence* of God and His love to others. We have a lot to do, as the acts of kindness we can perform are unlimited!

Have a blessed day

September 2

As I sit and have my cup of coffee with Jesus, I was reflecting on the word mercy. The dictionary defines MERCY as compassion or forgiveness shown toward someone who it is within one's power to punish or harm. Throughout the Bible, the word MERCY is often used. Jesus refers to it many times.

Luke 6:36 says, "Be merciful, just as your Father is merciful." Titus 3:5 says, "He saved us, not because of righteous things we have done, but because of HIS MERCY." And Hebrews 4:16 says, "Let us then approach God's throne of grace with confidence, so that we may receive MERCY and find grace to help us in our time of need." God shows us endless MERCY and asks us to do the same to each other.

Today, I am going to strive to be more MERCIFUL. I am going to reflect on the gift of one of my favorite devotions, the DIVINE MERCY, which says, "Jesus, I trust in you." We are so blessed to have a MERCIFUL God.

Have a beautiful day!

September 3

As I sit and have my cup of coffee with Jesus, I was thinking of the word *understanding*. I realize I do not understand all the ways in which God works, so I must *trust* Him. His ways are not our ways! I have to trust that there are no details in my life that are hidden from the Father.

Oftentimes, I must remind myself that God did not create me to understand these things, but to *know, love, and serve* Him! That helps me to live just for today and to center my day on him. I often want to control, to make things happen, and yet His will is perfect!

Today, I am going to live in His trust and promises. I'm going to live joyfully and peacefully in the day that He has made for me. I will handle only today, whatever sacred interruptions come, and trust that they are part of the heavenly plan.

Have a blessed day and enjoy His plans for you!

September 4

As I sit and have my cup of coffee with Jesus, I was thinking of the phrase *out of sync*. Sometimes, you wake up and, as you go through your day, you feel out of sync. From the very beginning, it feels like you are swimming upstream. On days like that, it's important to get centered, to find that place where the Spirit can bring balance.

Taking a moment to take a deep breath and to invite Jesus back into the situation can bring the Holy Spirit; this can snap you back in sync! I say often that we need to *slow down, simplify, and sanctify*. This is something we can practice every day to bring ourselves into the presence of Jesus!

Today, I am going to stay in sync. I'm going to allow the Holy Spirit to guide my day and to slow down, simplify, and sanctify this day.

Have a blessed day going with the flow.

September 5

As I sit and have my cup of coffee with Jesus, I was thinking of a phrase that Mother Teresa said, "I see God in every human being. When I wash the leper's wounds, I feel I am nursing the Lord himself." Is that not a beautiful expression? When I was going to an appointment the other day, I saw a homeless woman on the street. I wish I could say that I pulled over and ministered to her needs, but I caught myself wanting to ignore her. I've seen her many times before; what happened to my empathy and compassion?

It's easy to become frustrated when it seems our streets are becoming crowded with homeless people and complain about them, but when did we stop seeing Jesus in others? Mother Teresa is a great reminder that He is present in them! When we can see Jesus in every one of our brothers and sisters, when we don't see race, poverty, sex, or class, we can restore order and peace to our world.

Today, I am going to look for Jesus in everyone I encounter. And I am going to ask for the grace to see the Lord's face in each of them and offer them dignity, love, and peace!

Have a wonderful day encountering Jesus!

September 6

As I sit this morning and have my cup of coffee with Jesus, I decided to change positions, so instead of sitting, I laid on my back to look up at the clouds. The more I focused on the clouds, the more

I began to move outside of myself. From this view, the world seemed so much bigger and more safe.

I started thinking about my parents and my brother and sister living on the other side of those clouds. I began to see different forms and images, and for just a few moments, the problems of the world seem to disappear. God seemed to be so much larger than what we have made God to be.

We all need moments like this, when we get out of our own thoughts and just allow God to show us His *divine mystery*. Today, I am going to remember that I need to look up. I need to realize that God is so much bigger than I imagine. Today, I am going to be a part of the *divine mystery*.

Have a blessed day and look up!

September 7

As I sit and have my cup of coffee with Jesus, I was thinking about *miracles*. I have been very blessed in my life to see true miracles. I have seen people healed of cancer, people believed to be brain-dead come back to life, marriages healed, forgiveness take place. Often, we think the day of miracles was strictly for the Bible, but *miracles* are happening every day in our own lives.

When we slow down, we can see these miracles. When we go back and reflect, we can see the personal miracles God has placed in our lives and relationships. When we use the eyes of *faith*, we can see how God is moving His world and giving us physical, spiritual, and emotional miracles.

Today, as I go through the day, I'm going to look for miracles, some small and some big, and I'm going to take a few minutes to reflect on the miracles that God has performed in my life.

Miracle Day is a day full of blessings!

September 8

As I sit and have my cup of coffee with Jesus, I was reflecting on the power of the *name* of Jesus! Scriptures remind us that His name contains power. John 14:13 says, "Whatever you ask in my *name*, this I will do, that the Father may be glorified in the Son." How often do we truly rely on Him? How often do we call out His name?

Romans 10:13 says, "Everyone who calls on the name of the Lord will be saved." His is not a name like every other name. It is often taken in vain, but to one who believes and trusts in Him, it becomes power in a world of darkness.

Today, I am going to call upon His name. I am going to trust His Word. I will *live* His promises! I will feel the power of God as I call on the name of Jesus. Isn't it great to know that when you're sad or attacked and the world seems dark, all we need to do is to call on His *name* and He will be there!

Have a blessed day and call upon the name of Jesus. He is waiting!

September 9

As I sit and have my cup of coffee with Jesus, I was thinking of the word *hope*. I think how each one of us who call ourselves Christian needs to bring hope into our troubled world, the world filled with disease, fires, storms, and flooding. The list is endless. It's easy to give in to despair.

But Jesus came into the world to bring the Good News and *hope*. Every time we have a positive attitude, every time we pray for our world, every time we get out of bed, put a smile on our faces, and look for the blessings of the world, we bring *hope*.

Today, I am going to be the messenger of *hope* that our world needs. I'm going to look beyond all the negativity and be positive. Instead of tearing down, I will build up. I will take my attitude of gratitude and show the world that Jesus is *the* Good News. Can you imagine what would happen, not only in our homes and our country, but in our world, if we all brought that *hope* to the world!

Be an ambassador of hope! Have a blessed day!

September 10

As I sit and have my cup of coffee with Jesus, I was thinking about the song that woke me up this morning. The song was "Lean on Me" by Bill Withers. That should be the theme song for our relationship with Jesus. I reflected at the many times I have actually leaned on Him, and He was always there to carry me through.

It doesn't matter if we're going through a difficult time or if everything is wonderful, all we must do is lean on Him. In difficult times, with natural disasters, political upheaval, disease, and economic crisis, all of our world needs to lean on Him!

Today, as I am beginning my day, I just had Alexa play it again. "Lean on Me." And I just picture Jesus standing there with open arms, saying, "Lean on Me...that is all you need!" Today, I'm going to accept the grace that comes with leaning on and trusting in Him.

Have a great day, and don't forget to lean on Jesus. And if you need to, you can fall into His arms!

September 11

As I sit and have my cup of coffee with Jesus today, I was reflecting on a quote a friend sent me from Saint Padre Pio. Padre Pio said, "In the meantime, don't worry to the point of losing your inner peace. Pray with perseverance, with faith, with calmness and serenity."

September 11 brought fear and anxiety into our world, anxiety that has continued. But we need to listen to the words of this saint. We need to hold on to our inner peace, to remain prayerful, and to persevere. Yes, there is evil in the world, but with faith, we can bring the presence of God to a world that desperately needs it and restore *peace*!

Today, I will remember; the lives lost on 9/11. I will *not* forget. But I will also refuse to live in fear and lose the Father's *peace*! God will destroy evil. We cannot give into fear! I will remain prayerful and will persevere.

Have a blessed day and remember, we *trust* in Him!

September 12

As I sit and have my cup of coffee with Jesus, I celebrate this day. This was the day I was ordained a priest. I followed Jesus's voice and call, and He gave me a great journey. Although I did choose to leave, one day when the truth is out, people may understand my choice. But it really doesn't matter, as I followed Jesus.

But the beauty of this day is my recommitment to serve Christ. He has carried me through so much and yet has made Himself so present in guiding me in my new life. We all need to listen to His voice. It may take us to places we never dreamed of, but the journey is amazing and freeing. When we remember who we follow, when we remember who guides our lives, we can find His peace!

So today, I am grateful for all the wonderful people I have served and met on the journey and pray for those who try to destroy God's plan. It is a great day to celebrate a God that has a plan for each of us.

Sending blessings!

September 13

As I sit and have my cup of coffee with Jesus, I was reflecting on how important it is for us to have a *positive attitude*. It is true that everyone goes through difficult times, but we must keep our eyes fixed on Christ. Philippians 3:13–14 says, "Just one thing; forgetting what lies behind, straining forward to what lies ahead, I continue my pursuit toward the goal, the prize of God's upward calling in Christ Jesus."

We have nothing to worry about when we keep our eyes focused on Jesus and we make our *attitude* one of *gratitude* and peace. We can change the direction in which our world is going, but *we* must change first.

Today, let's bring an attitude of joy, peace, and love into a world that so desperately needs it. We can make a difference by keeping our eyes fixed on the prize, which is Jesus Christ.

Have a beautiful day!

September 14

As I sit and have my cup of coffee with Jesus, I was thinking about how *sacred* every day is. Though I do not know what today has in store, I believe it is all part of God's perfect plan. Therefore, it is *sacred*. From my quiet time with coffee and prayer to all the things to do today to the people I encounter, all is *sacred*.

When we can see the sacredness in our day, we encounter God! We can enter His presence while driving, talking on the phone, at work, or relaxing. We can encounter God with our families and our friends. The goal is to encounter Him! Slow down enough to see the *sacredness* in each moment.

Today, I am going to look deep and far and encounter God in my daily walk. I am going to be aware of His presence in my daily tasks. I am going to breathe deeply and allow Him to make me a part of His sacredness today!

Have a *sacred* and blessed day!

September 15

As I sit and have my cup of coffee with Jesus, I was reflecting on the word *celebrate*. Even when, as a community, we are going through so much—disease, violence, riots, politics, things which wreak *fear*—I choose to think about the word *celebrate*.

It's important for us to *celebrate*, first and foremost, our faith in Christ. He is the light that will bring us through the darkness. We can celebrate this morning, a new day with all kinds of opportunities. We celebrate relationships; in gratitude, we thank God for the people in our lives. We celebrate birthdays, anniversaries, graduations, a new school year. Instead of looking for all the things we can complain about, we need to celebrate all the *blessings* we have.

Today, let's celebrate the men and women who put their lives on the front lines, the police, sheriff, Highway Patrol, those in the armed services, those fighting fires, and those who teach our children, striving to learn new ways to reach them. When we *celebrate*, we *remember*, and when we *remember*, we *understand*, and when we understand *in gratitude*, we *celebrate*!

Have a blessed day, and remember, there is so much to *celebrate*.

September 16

As I sit and have my cup of coffee with Jesus, I was reflecting on the *voices* we hear. I remember growing up watching cartoons, and occasionally, there would be a character with a little devil on one side and a little angel on the other, and the character would hear both voices. Today, we hear many voices. We hear voices when we watch the news, we hear voices through social media, we hear voices in our heads, but the only voice we should strive to hear is God's.

Each day, we need to be *still* and *listen* for the voice of God. Scriptures tell us that He speaks to us in a whisper, in silence, in the heart, and it is important to take a moment to breathe deeply, clear the mind, and *listen* for His voice. Only when we hear His voice do we experience a *peace* that is like no other.

Today, as I begin my day, I will take time to be still, to be quiet, and to listen to His voice, which speaks to me from the beginning, and continues to draw my soul to Him! He says in Psalms 46, "Be still and know that I am God!" Be aware of the many voices that will strive to get your attention, today, but *listen* to His voice!

Have a blessed day!

September 17

As I sit and have my cup of coffee with Jesus, I was reflecting on a quote that someone posted yesterday. It said, "Every miracle in the Bible first started out as a problem." That is really *good news*! Think about any problem you have going on right now and know that it's the making of a miracle.

I'll bet if we went back and looked at our lives with its many problems, we would see many *miracles*, prayers that were answered, problems that were solved, ways in which God's hand was at work. All we have to do is *trust* that God is using the problems we are facing to perform miracles. If He can take water and turn it into wine, choice wine, if He can take Lazarus and *raise* him from the dead, then He can turn our problems *into* miracles!

Today, I put my trust in Jesus. Today, I name and give Him the problems I face, and I see a potential *miracle*. In fact, yesterday, I witnessed three of those miracles. From now on, I want to see every problem as a miracle *in the making*!

Have a miraculous day!

September 18

As I sit and have my cup of coffee with Jesus, I was thinking of the word *inspirational*. Throughout our lives, there have been many people who have inspired us, people who taught us about life, taught us how to be positive, and how to make a difference. It's good for us to remember those people; they remind us how important it is to have a relationship with the Lord.

So look back into your history at those people who *inspired* you, who saw the *good in you*, and who helped you succeed. Who are the people who gave you hope and who help lead you on the right path? If possible, call them or drop them a note, and remind them how much they mean to you. Pray for them today, whether living or passed on. Thank the Lord for the gifts they shared with you and realize that we are called to share those gifts with others. Our world needs people to inspire and not tear down, to bring hope and not despair. As Christians, we are called to this role.

Today, thank God for the people who brought inspiration to your life. Pay it forward, be an inspiration, bring a positive outlook into our world. Stop complaining, and start *inspiring*.

Have an inspirational day!

September 19

As I sit and have my cup of coffee with Jesus, I was thinking about *electricity*. Yesterday, a transformer in our neighborhood blew out, and we were without electricity for about six hours. It's amazing what you can't do without electricity—no TV, no AC, no Wi-Fi, no appliances. A couple neighbors and I sat out on the front porch and just talked. We connected and found that human connection is even better than the Internet!

It is the same way with Jesus. Unless we connect with Him, nothing really works. Now is a great time to make time for Jesus. After all, the toaster looks good, but unless you plug it in and turn it on, you don't get toast. To connect with Jesus, we have to make time for him.

Today, whether you're going to complete some things on your to-do list, visit with a friend, or get caught up on work, stay connected to Jesus. Invite Him into your day and stay plugged in. It's all about the connection!

Have a blessed day staying connected, plugged in, energized, and in the Lord!

September 20

As I sit and have my cup of coffee with Jesus, I have decided to make this "Let Your Light Shine Day!" When you begin your day with Jesus and invite Him to be a part of it, your light *shines*. Then it becomes your responsibility to let that light *shine* to our world.

We can do this in so many ways. We can put a smile on our faces and bring joy to a troubled world. We can call friends and check on them. We can take time to pray for others. We can discuss Jesus with our children. We can make some goodies and deliver them to somebody who may be alone. We can clean out our closets and give to the poor. We can take some time of silence and be grateful for all that God has done in our lives. That's what it means to *let your light shine*.

So today is "Let Your Light Shine Day!" Bring the *light* of Christ to others and may the joy you experience draw you closer to Him.

Have a great day!

September 21

As I sit and have my cup of coffee with Jesus, I was thinking about an old TV series called *Father Knows Best*. I think this applies to our spiritual life, for the Father does know best. He knows what we want, and He always gives us what we *need*.

Just think about today. The Father has plans for us. He wants us to experience His presence, to know His love and mercy. He gives us free will so that we can freely choose. And the question becomes what will we choose? Will we choose to think what is best for us, or will we trust that *the* Father *knows best*?

Today, I am going to strive to let the Father direct my day, my thoughts, and my actions. I am going to trust that the Father knows best. When I live in His presence and trust in His ways, my life becomes complete. And He shows me the *way*.

Today, trust that the Father *knows best* and relax! And have a great day.

September 22

As I sit and have my cup of coffee with Jesus, I was thinking of a conversation I had with friends yesterday. We came up with the expression to *splurge* or *purge*. When we find ourselves *splurging*, we collect more things. It can lead us to be more focused on self. It can take us away from our spiritual journey.

But when we *purge*, we simplify things. When we clean out our houses or storage units, we purge ourselves from attachment to things. When we purge ourselves from unnecessary activities, like watching too much news or useless television, we can find more time to study God's Word and make time to pray. Purging helps us to think about others and remain detached.

Today, I am going to focus on *purging* instead of *splurging*. I'm going to *simplify* so I can *intensify*. I'm going to allow the Holy Spirit to guide me on the path of finding *time* and *space* for our Lord.

Have a great day!

September 23

As I sit and have my cup of coffee with Jesus, I was thinking how important it is to do *one thing at a time*. Oftentimes, I would be proud that I could multitask, even sometimes triple task, if that is a word. The problem was, I was never *present* at any of them. I read somewhere, "one pleasure at a time." When I do one thing and I'm present, it's amazing how much better I do.

It's important to stay focused, to be attentive to what you are doing, thinking, or acting upon. You can begin today by being *calm* and thinking of all the blessings that God is giving you. In each task you do, *focus* on that before you move on to the next. We must let go of the *urgency* of everything and peacefully approach each person, task, and responsibility we have.

Today, I'm going to do one thing at a time. Right now, I'm taking a sip of coffee. Then I'm going to watch the sun come out and greet the new day with a good attitude, with *thanksgiving*.

Have a blessed day!

September 24

As I sit and have my cup of coffee with Jesus, I was thinking of the words *grief* and *gratitude*! They do not seem to go together, but I think they really do. In grief, we are deeply missing the love that filled our lives with joy. The pain when someone passes, however, can be overwhelming, and we forget the key element of *gratitude*! In our hearts, we are truly grateful to have experienced that *love*, no matter the pain. In moments of *grief*, I turn to *gratitude* for the great memories and love shared.

Just this morning, I was missing my family, my mother and father, both brothers, and my sister, who left this world too young. The grief is real, but the love and memories are real, too. I would rather have had the love and memories in my life than to have never experienced them at all. I also trust in God's promise that we will be together again.

So in the meantime, I wait patiently for the great reunion. *Grief and gratitude are alike*, even if they don't seem to be. You know, peanut butter and jelly are an unlikely pair, and yet they go together too.

Have a grateful day.

September 25

As I sit and have my cup of coffee with Jesus, I was thinking about how life keeps *moving forward*. Every day is a new beginning. We have to have *hope* and trust and move forward. It would be dangerous to drive a car always looking only in the rearview mirror. And it is dangerous to live life always looking backward.

Moving forward often takes *detachment*. Moving forward can be painful, as we see things with greater clarity and less glitter. Moving forward means trusting in God's *perfect* plan. Moving forward means to have a new excitement that wonderful things and miracles are just around the corner.

Today, I'm going to look forward with faith, hope, and love. I am going to embrace the past and the lessons I have learned while looking forward with *hope* and *trust*. I am going to allow God's Word, the sacraments, many friendships, and the *present moment* be my guide.

Have a blessed day and keep looking forward to the future. It is an eternal life with Jesus!

September 26

As I sit and have my cup coffee with Jesus, I was watching the *seasons change*. Some of the leaves on my trees are beginning to yellow, turn red, and fall to the ground. There's a crispness in the air. Fall decorations have come out, and it makes me aware that there are not just changes in nature, but *change* in ourselves, too.

The change of the seasons helps me reflect on the changes I've experienced in my life, the joys, the sorrows, the trials, the achievements, and the ups and downs of daily life. Seasons remind me that change is good. It makes things new; it renews. Revelation 21:5 says, "Behold, I make all things new."

Maybe it is time for us to welcome change not with fear, but with excitement and spirit. It's happening all around us every day. The sun just came up and birds are welcoming a new day. The seasons invite us to change. A new season of our lives has come. Let us embrace it and find Christ present in it!

Have a blessed day full of change!

September 27

As I sit and have my cup of coffee with Jesus, I was thinking about the word *enough*. In our world, it always seems like we need more, more money more time, more time off, even more time to spend with God! But the reality is God always gives us *enough*. It is what we do with it that is the problem. To begin our day in prayer, in reflection, and in surrender means that we have to take some of the *enough* time and apply it. Sometimes, we have to say *enough* to the things we waste time on.

Every day, God provides us with what we need, and it is *enough*. My mother used to say, "Enough of that, enough worrying, enough complaining!" What she meant was that's all...move on. Just today, God is providing us with enough, enough time, enough love, enough means to be the best version of ourselves. It becomes our choice to live in *enough*.

So today, I'm going to live in the *now*, with *enough*. I'm going to be grateful and patient and know that *enough* is *enough*.

Have a blessed day, knowing that one day is enough!

September 28

As I sit and have my cup of coffee with Jesus, I was reflecting on the word *surrender*. This word comes to me often, but it is not easy for people like me who like to control. For two years now, I have prayed a novena called the Surrender Novena. It has a powerful phrase at the end of each day which says, "O Jesus, I surrender myself to You. You take care of everything!"

Sometimes, we must surrender so that we can be strong. If we truly believe that God has a perfect plan and that He *is the* Lord of our life, then we must trust that whatever comes our way is part of His plan for our salvation. We may wish that things were different or not understand why we're going through certain trials, but we must trust in God's plan.

Today, we can enter another day with nothing to worry about as long as we take the hand of Jesus and listen to His voice. Surrender the need to make things happen and let them happen according to His will.

Have a blessed day, living in His presence and surrendering to your Lord!

September 29

As I sit and have my cup of coffee with Jesus, I was thinking of the word *see*. Yesterday, I was driving downtown, and I saw a woman with a white cane. She was blind. At the light, I was amazed to see how she maneuvered off the curb and across the crosswalk to get to the other side safely. I don't think I have ever thought much about my own *sight* or thanked God for the gift of it. It's one of the many blessings that we take for granted!

Then I began thinking a little more. It's not just the ability to *see* but rather what I am looking at. As I continued driving, I saw a homeless man walking in the middle of the street. I asked myself, "Do I *see* Jesus?" I realized I had already judged him. As I went home, I drove my regular route, and yet for the first time, I saw everything as new.

Today, I am grateful for the gift of *sight*, and I ask Jesus to take off my blinders, to help me to see Him in each person, to acknowledge the beauty of His creation, and to be grateful that I can *see*! Genesis 16:13 says, "You're the God who *sees* me!"

Have a blessed day!

September 30

As I sit and have my cup of coffee with Jesus, I was thinking of the word *faithfulness*. When you look up the word *faithfulness*, you see words like *loyal, constant,* and *steadfast*. I realize that, in my own life, I am not always faithful to the Lord. I question Him, I doubt Him, and sometimes, I don't trust Him!

But then, I realize the most important thing is that He is always *faithful* to me. That is the relationship that Jesus wants with us. He is always guiding us to a deeper level of *faithfulness* and trust in the Father. It's good to know that even when I may not be *faithful*, He is!

Today, I am going to begin by renewing my day with a recommitment to Him. I'm going to pledge my love and devotion and service to the Lord. Today, I will strive to remain *faithful* to the one who is always *faithful* to me.

Have a blessed day!

October 1

As I sit and have my cup of coffee with Jesus, I was reflecting on the word *true*. The word *true* means existing in *fact*, not merely as a possibility. In this day and age, it's really hard to determine what *true* is. There are so many voices talking on so many platforms that what is true is often blurred.

But Philippians 4:8–9 says, "Finally, brothers and sisters, whatever is *true*, whatever is honorable, whatever is just, whatever is pure, whatever is lovely, whatever is gracious, if there is any excellence, and if there is anything worthy of praise, think about these things. Keep on doing what you have learned and received and heard and seen in Me. Then the God of peace will be with you."

If we are going to search out the *truth*, we don't need to listen to the news, to Google, or to any social media, we just need to turn to God's Word. That is where we will find *truth*. What Jesus tells us is true! Today, take a moment, open your scriptures, and seek the *truth*.

Have a blessed day!

October 2

As I sit and have my cup of coffee with Jesus, I was thinking about the word *generosity*. Generosity begins by being aware that we have been given so much by our Lord! Think about the generosity of the Father. Think about all the times that He has raised you up. Think of all of the things He has given you in this lifetime. Think about the people that He has brought into your life to lift you up. And think about John 3:16, "For God so loved the world that He gave His only begotten Son, that whoever believes in Him shall not perish, but have eternal life!"

We can be generous because we have a God who has taught us to be giving firsthand. Today, let's recognize the many blessings we receive and share those with others in the spirit of *generosity*. God is already generous in giving us a new day; let us rejoice and be glad in it.

Have a blessed day, and happy feast day of the *guardian angels*!

October 3

As I sit and have my cup of coffee with Jesus, I was reflecting on living in the *present moment*. Right now, it's still dark outside. I can hear the trains behind me in the far distance. I can hear the traffic. I look forward to hearing the birds come out and to seeing the sun rise. I look forward to the neighbors going by and waving. I look forward to the world waking up. But I still want to be in the *present moment*.

There are times when we experience something special, like the beautiful ocean or a spectacular mountain or a magnificent sunrise; those are extra special moments. If only we could stay at these places where we find God, but we were not made to stay there. These special times are simply meant to be moments of *inspiration*! We need to find that place of peace in the day-to-day chores, the everydayness of washing dishes, cleaning the yard, or driving, because our God lives in them.

On this beautiful morning, I am going to strive to be *present* in the *moment*! I'm going to strive to see God in my everyday activities. I'm always grateful for those special moments where He reveals Himself in a unique way, but we grow when we can see Him in every *moment*. Look for Him today. He *is* right in front of you!

Have a blessed day!

October 4

As I sit and have my cup of coffee with Jesus, I was reflecting on the life of St. Francis. Today is his feast day. I have always felt very close to this special saint. I was blessed to serve Saint Francis Parish for more than twenty years, and I have made over forty visits to Assisi, where Francis lived in Italy. Even my middle name is Francis!

Francis was an amazing person, embracing a life with only one purpose, to point others to Christ. That is the purpose we all share. One of the basic precepts of our Catechism says that our purpose is to *know*, *love*, and *serve* God! In our daily walk, we must ask ourselves what we are doing to better know, love, and serve Him.

To know Him means to study His Word, *to pray*, and to seek a relationship with Him! To *love* Him means to spend time with Him and to *listen* to Him. To *serve* Him means to put the lives of others before our own!

Have a blessed day. Saint Francis, pray for us!

October 5

As I sit and have my cup of coffee with Jesus, I was thinking about the battle between *faith* and *fear*. In the crazy world we live in today, it seems that fear can creep in and take over. Call it fear, anxiety, worry—it's all the same!

Samuel Rutherford once said, "The secret formula of the saints is: when I am in the cellar of affliction, I look for the Lord's choicest wines." And Norman Vincent Peale said, "Worrying is accepting the responsibility that God never intended you to have!" So there is really nothing for us to worry about; we must *trust* in the Lord.

Today is a great opportunity for us to *surrender* all our *worries* and our *fears* and trust in Jesus. It is going to be a great day because God has all kinds of wonderful plans for us.

Be happy, *don't* worry! And have a blessed day.

October 6

As I sit and have my cup of coffee with Jesus, I was thinking about the word *knowledge*. When we let ourselves be guided by truth, we gain knowledge. Each of us learns lessons in our own time. On our journey, we have to go at our own pace while letting others go at theirs. Jesus is working in our lives daily to show us where we need to change and grow, to teach us to love more, to trust more, to be more alive.

Today, I am going to let myself and others do things at their own pace. I will slow down enough to experience the blessings and challenges of the day. I will listen for the voice of Jesus and follow His guidance. I will trust Him and let Him set the pace. I will not compare my journey with that of others, but will live in the *present moment*, listening to Jesus and letting Him guide me!

Have a blessed day!

October 7

As I sit and have my cup of coffee with Jesus, I was thinking of the *power of the spoken word*. Being given the gift of speech, we have the power to lift people up or to destroy them with our words. I read a quote from a philosopher, Zeno, who said, "Better to trip with the feet than with the tongue." He goes on to say that we can always get up after we fall, but must remember that what we have said can never be unsaid, especially if it is cruel or hurtful. And James 1:19 says, "Everyone should be quick to listen, slow to speak, and slow to become angry."

When we follow Jesus, we learn to control what we say. Sometimes in anger and frustration, we say things we don't mean. From the same mouth, we can praise our God one moment and yet tear down another human being the next.

Today, let us strive to be followers of Jesus, careful of what we say so that we can build up His kingdom!

Have a blessed day!

October 8

As I sit and have my cup of coffee with Jesus, I was reflecting on the word *embrace*, which means to support, to welcome, or to hold closely in one's arms. You might remember that during the pandemic, it was recommended that we stay six feet apart. That was devastating There were many grandparents missing the embrace of their grandchildren and loved ones often died in the hospital alone. But because we were not able to embrace others, it led many to embrace the Lord. And He always embraces us!

In Ecclesiastes 3:5, it says, "There is a time to throw stones and a time to gather stones; a time to *embrace* and a time to shun embracing." Not even a pandemic could keep our Lord from *embracing us*!

Today, take a moment in prayer, close your eyes, and feel the arms of our Lord around you. His *embrace* brings you peace, security, and love. *Embrace* the day, *embrace* the trials, *embrace* the *blessings*, and know that you are not alone!

Have a blessed day!

October 9

As I sit and have my cup of coffee with Jesus, I was reflecting on the gift of *waiting*. Time is such an important and valuable part of our lives. We spend a lot of our time *waiting*—waiting in traffic, waiting in line, waiting to hear from a friend, waiting to finish an exam; the list goes on and on. We cannot deny that *waiting* is a part of that valuable time.

But *waiting* is an art. We must learn to *wait patiently*, knowing that God's plan is unfolding in perfect time. The scriptures are full of people who waited patiently for God to reveal His plan. Abraham and Sarah waited to have a child they so longed for. Noah waited for the waters to recede. Paul waited in the prison cells. And we, too, are invited to wait for God's perfect timing. We may get restless or uncomfortable, but we need to deal with our frustrations by learning to practice the *art of waiting*.

Today, I am going to practice the art of *waiting* joyfully. I'm going to trust that God is working in each and every area of my life for His glory. Waiting doesn't mean I can't continue to live in His presence. It just means He has a greater plan, and He wants me to trust Him!

Have a blessed day!

October 10

As I sit and have my cup of coffee with Jesus, I was reflecting on the scripture verse from Philippians 4:6 that says, "Do not be *anxious* about anything!" Oftentimes, we wake up already stressed out before the day even begins. We rush through our day saying, "When this is over, then I'll pray" or "Then I'll rest." But it never happens. Wouldn't it be nice to not be anxious about anything?

We need to begin our day by handing our anxiety, our worries, and our entire *life* over to Jesus. It's all in our minds. We need to turn our *anxiety* into *excitement*! We have the power to live today with great excitement and positivity or to create worry, anxiety, and negativity. Just think, each day is a new day, a brand-new day, to learn new things, to see new things, and to experience God's love.

So make today a great day. Whatever you do, do it with a smile. Wherever you go, keep your eyes in the moment and see God's creation in all. And whoever you encounter, know that you are encountering Christ face-to-face. Jesus reminds us that we *don't* have to be anxious about anything when we walk with Him.

Have a blessed day!

October 11

As I sit and have my cup of coffee with Jesus, I was thinking about a reflection I read. In it was a quote that said, "Give me the courage to *budge* whenever you *nudge*." How often does God nudge us? He puts a person in our minds that He wants us to reach out to. He puts a thought in our heads of a kindness we can do. He nudges us. And how often do we ignore it?

It's a great day to think about what God is *nudging* us to do. He nudges us to open our eyes to the beauty of His creation. He *nudges* us to reach out to someone who is sick or alone. He *nudges* us to spend some quiet time in prayer. Listen to the soft whisper of His holy voice, and when God *nudges*, have the courage to *budge*!

And have a blessed day.

October 12

As I sit and have my cup of coffee with Jesus, I was thinking of *darkness*. It's 4:10 in the morning, so it's pretty dark outside. A few people have their lamps on in the window, but other than that, it's dark. Sometimes in our lives, we find ourselves in darkness, even when it's bright and sunny outside.

Many people can find themselves in very dark and sad places. That's when they must remember the sunrise! The *light* is there, just ready to come out and bring us bright *hope* and *peace*! We must remember that this, too, will pass, and we will be in His *light*. We must just patiently wait and trust. So when going through a dark period, remember that Jesus, the *light*, will shine. And we wouldn't appreciate the *light* if we never experienced the darkness.

Today, I will wait for the *light*. I *know* it is coming. I think I love this time of the morning best when out of the darkness, it becomes *light*. Then I can see so much more than I ever saw in the dark. As I sit here and reflect, my street is coming alive. More lights are coming on, people are getting up, and soon, the *sun* will be shining.

Have a blessed day, basking in the *light*!

October 13

As I sit and have my cup of coffee with Jesus, I was thinking of the word *yield*. You do not see that word very often, but while driving the other day, I came up to a sign that said *yield*. I had to stop and think for a moment and remember that the definition of *yield* is to give way!

I often find myself in such a hurry that I fail to *yield* to what God is asking me to do. I need to practice the art of yielding to God's plan in my life so that I am not rushing full speed ahead into my own. Scriptures tell me His *ways* are not my ways. It is important that I *yield* when I come to an intersection, and it is important that I *yield* to the plans of Christ.

Today, as I go through the day, I will focus on yielding, *yielding* to the needs of others, *yielding* to my family, and most importantly, *yielding to* the voice of God! I have personally seen what happens when you *don't* yield. It always ends up in disaster.

Have a beautiful day.

October 14

As I sit and have my cup of coffee with Jesus, I was thinking about the importance of *praying for others*. I find it easy to pray for my own personal needs, asking God for help in my own life. And it's easy for me to pray for people who've asked for my prayers, for my family, for my church, for the sick, and for those who have died. I also like to expand my prayer to universal prayer, praying for the world, for peace and unity. The one I struggle with is praying for those who have hurt me or who have attacked me…basically, praying for my enemies. That I find difficult.

But Jesus calls us to *pray* for our enemies. I don't have a lot of them, maybe just a handful of people, but it is still not easy to pray for them. Matthew 5:44 says, "But I say to you, love your enemies and *pray* for those who persecute you." Easier said than done. Following Jesus is not always the easiest thing to do, so today, I am going to pray for those who persecute me. I'm going to ask the Lord to remove the bitterness, the anger, and the hurt I feel and turn it into love, mercy, and forgiveness.

But I know myself. I'm probably going to have to read these words three or four times today to remind myself of what I have promised. If I am going to claim Jesus as my Lord, I must follow Him and His Word.

Have a wonderful day. And don't forget to pray for others.

October 15

As I sit and have my cup of coffee with Jesus, I was thinking of Saint Teresa of Avila. Today is her feast day. She said, "Let *nothing* disturb you, let *nothing* frighten you, though all things pass. God does *not* change. *Patience* wins all things. But he lacks nothing who possesses God; for God *alone* suffices."

What a wonderful reminder at the beginning of a day! We cannot let things disturb us or frighten us, because our God is with us. Whenever you feel under attack, overwhelmed, or anxious, the saints always remind us that there is power in Jesus.

Today, we surrender our worries, our fears, the pressures, the attacks, with the powerful words, "Oh, Jesus, I surrender myself to you. You take care of everything."

Have a very wonderful, blessed day! And Saint Teresa, pray for us!

October 16

As I sit and have my cup of coffee with Jesus, I was reflecting on the phrase, "God uses broken things." Throughout the scriptures, God has always used those people who are completely broken to fulfill His promises. Whether you have been *broken* emotionally, physically, or spiritually, God can use you. If you have been broken with your ambitions, finances, relationships, or worldly reputation, He needs you! Whether you are broken with health issues, mental illness, or addiction, God can still use you! In the Bible, we see that these are often the kinds of people God uses.

Each morning, as I begin my day with the Lord, I am aware of my own brokenness. At times, I draw inward, and I feel I want to throw myself a pity party. But then, as the Lord opens my heart, I realize He needed this brokenness for a greater plan. Don't get me wrong. I would rather be strong and in control, but evidently, that is not His plan.

Today, I am going to give my brokenness to the Lord so that He can piece together what He needs to make this world a better place. Just like the body of Christ must be broken before it can be shared, so it is with us. Today, do not be afraid. Allow God to use your brokenness to heal a broken world.

And have a blessed day!

October 17

As I sit and have my cup of coffee with Jesus, I was thinking about *slowing down*. Sometimes, it seems that time has slowed down so much that I don't even know what day it is until I wake up and look at my watch! And other times, it speeds up almost out of control.

We need to slow down and take a few moments to reconnect with our Creator. This doesn't cost a thing, but it gives everything! Sitting outside in a favorite chair watching the seasons change, taking the dog for a walk, watering the yard, baking something for someone, calling an old friend, or going for a drive are all times when you can really focus on God's handiwork. *Slowing down* should remind us about living in the *present* moment, enjoying the presence of God.

Today, there are some things I must do, but I am also going to consciously take time to *slow down* and acknowledge the presence of God!

Have a blessed day, and remember to slow down.

October 18

As I sit and have my cup of coffee with Jesus this morning, I was thinking about a quote I read somewhere that said, "More is accomplished by folding your hands than by wringing them." In other words, when we put our hands together in prayer, we can accomplish a lot more than when we just wring them in worry!

These days, it is easier for us to worry than it is for us to *trust*. Things of this world can certainly shake our lives and routines, but we have to believe that God is right there with prayer to connect us to Him. What are you worried about that you have not taken to God? Remember, God's office is always open 24/7!

Today, turn to the Son of God with your worries and fears. Get renewed, get excited, get fulfilled, for no day is ordinary with an extraordinary God.

Have a blessed day!

October 19

As I sit and have my cup of coffee with Jesus, I was thinking of a funny saying I heard that says, "God invites us to drop our burdens on Him! And unlike the dry cleaning, we don't have to pick them up again." Often in our daily walk, we hold on tightly to the past and what could have been. Then we worry about what the future will be. But Jesus wants us to focus on what is. Jesus calls us to make this day new and to walk in His light.

Whatever is holding you back, it is time to let it go and allow the Lord to use you. He will take your pain, your trials, and your fears, and with strong purpose, He will use it to build His kingdom. We don't need to keep dwelling on the past, and we don't need to look into the future. We need to live today. We need to make his *presence* known to our world through our unshakable faith.

Today is a great time to set the pace. We can leave our worries and fears behind and make today the best day of our lives. It's a choice. It's the right choice.

Have a blessed day!

October 20

As I sit and have my cup of coffee with Jesus, I was thinking about the many different types of prayers we pray. There are simple prayers children make, like "Jesus, I want a bicycle," and there are the complex inner yearnings of our souls, seeing God in mysterious, sacramental awareness. My mornings with Jesus contain a meditation on the rosary, praying the Divine Office, and different reflections that people have written. And sometimes, it is in just gazing at the sun rising and hearing the birds singing that I turn my prayer to praise.

Yesterday, when I went to pick up some water at a store, the parking lot was rather full. As I was walking into the store, a woman approached me and said that it was nice to see me and asked if I had a hard time finding parking. I responded, "Yes."

She said, "Try my prayer. Hail Mary, full of grace, help me find a parking place."

She said it worked every time.

So you see, prayer comes in all forms! Sometimes, we need to break out of our routine so that our prayer does not become just a mumbling of words. Basically, it is God present to us and us present to Him! Whatever way in which God speaks to your heart that you are open to, this is prayer. One form is not always better than the other, and you would be surprised at how many ways He can reach us. Today, may your prayer life be real and rich. May you look beyond and within. May you touch the finger of God.

Have a blessed day!

October 21

As I sit and have my cup of coffee with Jesus, I was thinking about *detachment*. When should we detach from people? When we are hooked into reacting with anger, fear, guilt, or shame? Is it when our mind gets focused on revenge, and we plot how to protect ourselves? This is when we need to think about detaching for a time, so we don't act out of pain, and let space and time help *heal* the issue.

What's most important is that we find our inner peace. Getting centered and restoring balance will help us. We can do practical things like breathing deeply or exercising. As we center ourselves, we can look at the issue differently. The Holy Spirit will guide us to a new approach.

Today, if someone or something makes you react in anger, fear, shame, or guilt, step back, center in the moment, and with God, let Him take you to a safe place where you can bring His peace into the situation. When you find this place, you will find the *peace* and the connection you need.

Have a blessed day.

October 22

As I sit and have my cup of coffee with Jesus, I was thinking about a saying a friend sent me yesterday. It says, "If the grass looks greener on the other side…stop staring. Stop comparing and stop complaining, and start watering the grass that you're standing on!" So often, we compare ourselves to others. We think their lives are easier or better than ours, but in reality, all life comes from God and all life is good. Even the difficult parts of life, like sickness and death, are just a continuation of life and life lessons God has planned for us.

Today, I'm going to start watering the grass that I'm standing on. I am going to work to stop comparing and complaining, for God has blessed me beyond measure. Every day, I strive to live in the present moment, focusing on what God is asking of me and listening for His voice.

Have a great day, and pray for help in accepting the life God has created for you.

October 23

As I sit and have my cup of coffee with Jesus, I decided to call this Don't Forget Him Day. Every day is a great day to recognize what God has done for us. We can look back with gratitude that we are here today. And we can look forward to what God has in store for us this day.

Today is your new beginning. Take time to renew yourself by *focusing* on the Father, *centering* on the Son, and *surrendering* to the Spirit! Put a smile on your face, a bounce in your step, and His Spirit in your heart!

Have a blessed day.

October 24

As I sit and have my cup of coffee with Jesus, I was thinking about the fact that God's grace is all we need. Sometimes we go through life looking back, saying, "What if..." or "If only..." But Jesus calls us to stay focused on His grace and His promises. In 2 Corinthians 12:9, it says, "My grace is sufficient for you!"

Look to the past as lessons learned rather than as a place to stay. Stop looking in the rearview mirror or you'll end up in a wreck! A friend of mine is famous for saying, "It is what it is!" Live in the present moment and ask the important questions: "What does the Lord want me to do today? How can I be more loving and forgiving today? What am I grateful for?"

Those are the questions that need to be answered. Leave the "what ifs" and the "if onlys" in the past where they belong. Today belongs to the Lord. He wants you to be a part of it!

Have a blessed day!

October 25

As I sit and have my cup of coffee with Jesus, I was thinking about how *fear* oftentimes dominates our lives. It drains us of the energy we need to enjoy this life. It blocks relationships and can even make us ill. *Fear* oftentimes keeps us from our relationship with Jesus. If we really believe God's Word and we open our hearts to Him, then we should have nothing to fear.

The *opposite* of *fear* is safety and *trust*. Fear is something that we play out in our minds. What we fear is usually not true. When we are living in the past or we are afraid of tomorrow, we can't live in the *present moment*. We cannot live in the present moment and live in fear at the same time. We cannot live in fear and yet *trust* in Jesus at the same time. The Divine Mercy teaches us to pray, "Jesus, I trust in You."

So today, on this beautiful morning, with the changing of the seasons, the day of the Lord, let us name our fears and *surrender* them to the Father. Let us make today about living in His presence, about worship and adoration, about love and peace! *Fear* is another four-letter word we need to remove from our vocabulary.

Have a blessed day. Don't worry. Be happy!

October 26

As I sit and have my cup of coffee with Jesus, I decided to call today a day to *make it meaningful*. We can give meaning to everything we do from the time we get up until we go to sleep. We can wake up with a smile and a heart full of gratitude for a new day, or we can wake up and complain about what we need to do. It's all about *attitude*.

Jesus invites us to make this day *meaningful*. We can change our whole day by just having a heart of *gratitude*. A kind act, a simple prayer for someone, gratefulness that we have things to do make all the difference. We can make driving to work meaningful as we talk to God about the day ahead. We can make tasks that we don't want to do meaningful by offering them up for someone who is going through a hard time.

Today, I'm going to give *meaning* to each moment throughout the entire day! I am going to praise God for the ordinary things as well as the extraordinary things. With gratitude and thanksgiving, I'm going to live this day with new opportunities and new adventures.

Happy Make It Meaningful Day!

October 27

As I sit and have my cup of coffee with Jesus, I decided to call it Take It to Him Day. That reminds me that I need to take to Him everything that is going on in my life. It's so easy to turn to other things to guide us. People turn to popular opinion, to counselors, to the news, to horoscopes, to psychics, to whatever else that is out there, but Jesus tells us to take it to Him!

When we take our worries, our fears, our frustrations, and our anger to Him, things begin to happen! That is why we always need to stay close to His scriptures, to study them, to search for answers, knowing that God's Word will guide us.

Proverbs 3:5–6 says, "Trust in the Lord with all your heart, on your own intelligence rely not. In all your ways be mindful of Him, and He will make straight your paths." Today, open His word, place it in your heart, and let Him be your guide. In other words, make it a Take It to Him Day!

Have a blessed day!

October 28

As I sit and have my cup of coffee with Jesus on this *beautiful day*, I was reflecting on James 4:8, which says, "Come near to God and He will come near to you." Do you find yourself sometimes saying, "As soon as I get this done or that done, I will make time for prayer?" Or "When I get my to-do list done, I will take time to be alone with the Lord." You will always find that the time just disappears. We need to make sure we make time for Jesus!

We can get distracted and move away from God because of the busyness of our day. But God never moves away from us. We need to slow down, especially with our time with the Lord. We can't rush through our prayer time, quiet time, or scripture reading.

Today, I am going to focus on being near to Him and at peace with Him. I will take the time to be in His presence.

Have a blessed day!

October 29

As I sit and have my cup of coffee with Jesus, I was reflecting on a G. K. Chesterton quote that someone sent me. It says, "In the struggle for existence, it is only those who hang on for ten minutes after all is hopeless, that *hope* begins to dawn."

In one way or another, we have all experienced hopelessness. We wonder if things will ever be normal again. Fear creeps, manifesting itself as worry or anxiety. But when we stay close to the Lord and hold on tightly to Him, hope begins to dawn!

Today is a new dawn. We need to pick ourselves up, brush ourselves off, put a smile on our faces, and approach this day with *hope*. Our whole demeanor needs to be one of spreading *hope*. Where there is *hope*, there is the Lord, and where there is the Lord, there is peace and joy!

Have a blessed day filled with *hope*!

October 30

As I sit and have my cup of coffee with Jesus, I was reflecting on the new coffee mug I got. It has a quote from Mother Teresa on it which says, "*Silence* gives us a new perspective!" Each day, we need to make time to sit and be silent. It is in these moments that God can speak to our hearts. In these moments, God can ease our pain, stop our minds from racing, and help us to see His plan for us.

Silence is not easy! We live in a world where there is always noise, activity, and distraction. A few moments of complete silence, breathing in and out, listening can open our souls and can connect us with our Lord.

Today, turn off the TV, turn off the radio, and put down the phone. Close your eyes and go to that place of *silence* where Jesus speaks to you. Silence gives us a new perspective, and it allows us to hear the whisper of God's voice!

Have a blessed day! And say a prayer for me…it's my birthday!

October 31

As I sit and have my cup of coffee with Jesus, I was thinking of the word *magnitude*! It's a powerful word, defined as a great size or extent of something. Everything that Jesus says or does has great magnitude. This is something we need to embrace.

When I *love* with great magnitude, *forgive* with great magnitude, and *live* with great magnitude, things begin to happen. With all the negativity that surrounds us, the answer is for us to produce a great positive magnitude of *love*. A kind word, patience, reaching out to someone else, all can bring a *magnitude* of love.

Today, I am going to live in the magnitude of God's love. I'm going to stop complaining, stop worrying, and allow the energy that God offers to control my life and my day. I am going to be drawn into His grace and spirit and allow it to flow through me to others. This way, we can create a great *magnitude* of love.

Have a great day!

November 1

As I sit and have my cup of coffee with Jesus this All Saints Day, I think of the wonderful examples that the saints have been to me. I have always had a great devotion to St. Francis and have, for over forty years, visited his home in Assisi. It's a special place where I always encounter Jesus. Padre Pio has always been an inspiration to me, how he endured persecution and yet stayed faithful to Jesus. Saint John Vianney, patron of priests, did not have it easy, but reminds me that when you hear the voice of God, you must follow Him.

So many saints have inspired me in my journey and some of them are still living. Friends who have battled cancer and done so with a great witness and testimony, friends who overcame addictions and continue today to witness freedom, priests and religious who are still the hands to feed the poor and serve God, all are living saints!

Today, we are reminded that we are called to be saints, called to endure, persevere, and embrace! In these tumultuous times, we need saints to stand up and remind us that Jesus is *alive* and well! Have a great day and look around. There may be a saint living under your own roof!

November 2

As I sit and have my cup of coffee with Jesus today, I think of the word *remember*. Today is All Souls Day, and in a special way, it's a time to remember all our family, friends, and people who have played an important part in our life and have *transitioned*. For anyone who has lost someone, it is a time to remember and reflect. I don't know how people survive without a relationship with Jesus Christ. I don't know how people survive without believing His Word about eternal life.

So today, take a moment, name their names, and *remember*. Feel the spirit and love, and know that, one day soon, we will be reunited. As you sit and take some quiet time to remember, realize you were *blessed* because they were a part of your life. Lots of tears will be shed today, but just think of the great reunion!

May the souls of the faithful departed through the mercy of God rest in peace.

Have a blessed day *remembering*!

November 3

As I sit and have my cup of coffee with Jesus, I was thinking about the word *obedience*. If you look in the scriptures, you will find that Jesus never forces or threatens *obedience*. Jesus uses *if*. "If anyone desires to come after Me, let him deny himself." This is true *discipleship*; He invites us to a life and encourages us to follow.

Jesus makes His way, His truth, and His life very clear; it's not about rules, it's about a way of life based on love, mercy, and forgiveness. This is something our world needs to see today more than ever. When we obey Jesus, God's love flows through us and touches the lives of many others. Forced obedience is controlling, and it's easy to fall into that sin.

Today, we should be asking ourselves if we are joyfully, willingly, and obediently following Jesus or are we living out of fear and control. If you're living out of fear and control, Jesus is not a part of it. Today, let's live in the freedom of being a true disciple, following Jesus. What a great day, *choosing* to be obedient to God's Word! Have a blessed day!

November 4

As I sit and have my cup of coffee with Jesus, I think of the words *divine timing*. It's amazing how I can try to manipulate time. I have a long to-do list, I keep a calendar, and of course, I think I know how things should progress. And then I ran into *divine timing*! It has an easy definition. It is God's timing, perfect timing!

When you go through difficult times or you feel like you are swimming upstream, when you wonder when will the pain stop, you have to connect with *divine timing*! Whatever God is doing in your life, He has a perfect plan, and His timing is perfect. Sometimes, we are called to *sacred waiting* and sometimes *sacred suffering*. But for God, it all has purpose. We need to say to ourselves, "This, too, shall pass." And while we wait, we have to trust in His Word that whatever we're going through is necessary for the building of His kingdom.

Divine timing is perfect timing, and it is what we need to become holy. So today, take a deep breath, get in sync with divine timing, and trust that whatever you're going through, God is using it to make you holy! Have a beautiful day!

November 5

As I sit and have my cup of coffee with Jesus, I'm thinking about *trust*. With so much uncertainty in the world, I keep going back to the word *trust*.

There is a lot of uncertainty in my life, and yet I must *trust* that Jesus has a perfect plan and perfect timing. I must let go and *surrender* to His plan and quit trying to control. Oh, how much I love control! But I do believe that when you trust Jesus, He will guide you, *no* matter how difficult it may seem. He will guide you to the truth.

So today, I say over and over the prayer of the Divine Mercy, "Jesus, I trust in you!" Have a blessed day, and remember, Jesus is the King!

November 6

As I sit and have my cup of coffee with Jesus, I was thinking of a conversation I had with a good friend yesterday. She is battling cancer, and we were talking about why we have to go through difficult times. She is very brave, and we were sharing about how we don't always understand why God allows suffering. Where is God when all of this is happening?

We discussed how God allowed Jesus to suffer. He offered that suffering up for us. We talked about the importance of that when we are afraid, in pain, or suffering to think of others, to get outside of our self. Hearing her vulnerability and trust in Jesus just reminded me how powerful our God is. We reminded each other that we all must stay close to Him and *trust* Him! I'm so grateful I have friends that fight the fight, and even though they have moments of fear, they just need to be reminded that Jesus is carrying them through this. I got off the phone, and I felt so empowered, so grateful!

Jesus, today, we offer to you any fear, any pain, any suffering. We surrender our lives to you and trust this is part of our journey to holiness. Have a blessed day!

November 7

As I sit and have my cup of coffee with Jesus, I was thinking about farmers and how much trust they have to place in God. Many parts of our world, including our valley, have had to deal with many droughts, and yet when the rain comes, it is a wonderful time to show gratitude for God. It cleans the air, replenishes the earth, and should remind us to thank God for the food we eat and the laborers who work the land. Give *praise* to God for the rain.

Sometimes, it is the simple things that we need to give *thanks* and *praise* to God for. It says in Acts 14:7, "He has shown kindness by giving you rain from heaven and crops in their seasons." He provides you with plenty of food and fills your heart with *joy*!

Today, I thank you, Lord, for always fulfilling your promises and reminding us that the greatest gift of praise is *thank you*! May this day be a time of renewal and *thanksgiving* for the simple things! Let the rain flow! Have a *blessed* day!

November 8

As I sit and have my cup of coffee with Jesus, I am thinking about *change*. *Change* is not easy. The seasons are changing. Even the way we worship is changing. School, family life, shopping, and social life are all changing. The one thing that is consistent is Jesus Christ.

We need to focus on the fact that we were created for one thing: to *know*, *love*, and *serve* Christ. Changes are happening; they are out of our control, but our relationship with Jesus is within our grasp. The most important thing *is* that we *change* ourselves. Today, let us move out of the fear of change into a personal relationship with Him! Have a blessed day!

November 9

As I sit and have my cup of coffee with Jesus, I was thinking about the word *anxiety*. I've had so many calls and emails from people telling me that they are full of anxiety. The Bible says *do not* be anxious about anything; Philippians 4:6 says, "Do not be anxious about anything, but in every situation, by prayer and petition, with *thanksgiving* make your request known to God!"

This is perfect advice for tumultuous times. Take time through your day to stop and take a deep breath and know that everything is in God's hands. Tell God what you're worried about, name it out loud, and then, with thanksgiving, hand it over to Him, trusting that He hears your prayers, and He will give you everything you need! I'm not sure why we always make it so hard. Jesus makes it very easy. We were not made to live in anxiety; we were made to live in trust in Jesus!

Have a wonderful day, let go of worry, and embrace the Lord's calming Spirit! He has not let you down yet!

November 10

As I sit and have my cup of coffee with Jesus, I was thinking about the word FOUNDATION. Foundations are very important. For some, we had parents who laid a very strong and healthy foundation for us; others had to build their own. Some people have been blessed to have had teachers, coaches, mentors, or spiritual leaders who helped to build a strong foundation.

Today is a great day to reflect on who helped build your foundation. Who helped you to get to where you are today? As Christians, we are blessed that JESUS has become our FOUNDATION. It's by HIS WORD that we build our lives. Our faith in HIM has become the cornerstone on which we build our lives today. It doesn't matter whether you started with a weak foundation or a strong one. What matters is that Christ is the cornerstone of that foundation, and not even Satan can touch that!

Have a beautiful day and take time to reflect on the foundation that holds you up!

November 11

As I sit and have my cup of coffee with Jesus, I think about the power of *breathing*. In the book of Genesis 2:7, it says that "The Lord our God formed man out of the dust of the ground and breathed life into his nostrils, the breath of *life*, and the man became a living creature."

Every time we pause to take a deep breath, we connect with that *first* breath. Our minds become clear, our hearts slow down, and we bring peace into the moment. We are so used to being in such a hurry, worrying about so many things that we forget the simple gift of *breath*.

Today, as you go through your day, as you get in your car, between appointments, take a moment and pause and take a deep *breath* and reconnect with God!

Have a blessed day centered in the breath of life!

November 12

As I sit and have my cup of coffee with Jesus, I'm thinking about how much God continues to take me out of my *comfort zone*. I like routine, I like ritual, I like things to go with order. But it seems these past few years, God is moving me out of my comfort zone.

Sometimes in our life, God needs us to move and to grow so that He can use us. Don't get me wrong, I don't like it at all, but when

I quiet myself and I sit in His presence, it is easier to *surrender*. He's never let me down in the past, and I must trust that He has a plan for me!

So today, I recommit my life to Jesus. I let Him take me where He needs me to be, and I graciously, and not so graciously at times, *follow*. Today, I'm going to say the word *trust*. Jesus, I *trust* in You many times and trust that God is taking me to a new comfort zone where I will encounter Him in a deeper and more profound way. Have a blessed day.

November 13

As I sit and have my cup of coffee with Jesus (and Francis), I think of the word *truth*! One of my good friends sent me a quote yesterday. It said, "Oftentimes, it is the built-up debris that causes us to go deeper, so we can search for the *truth*. Go deep, live life from the *truth* within, and watch your innate beauty manifest outward."

Today, what a time to go deeper into the *truth*. It is not a long conversation. You don't have to read books; it is just taking the time to quiet yourself and allow yourself to go inward to be one with Him.

Not *doing*, just *being*! Allowing His spirit to be one with yours. Today is another opportunity for us to seek the *truth*! May the *truth* shine through you and make this world a better place.

November 14

As I sit and have my cup of coffee with Jesus, I am thinking of the contrast between *light* and dark. When I get up each morning, it is really dark outside. Lately, it's been cold, so I've come inside to do my reflections. Darkness can be very profound in our lives. Sometimes, it comes with fear, sometimes depression, and even loneliness.

In contrast with the dark is the *light* of Jesus Christ. Even when it is dark, He is present. When we strive to look and move toward the *light*, we can move beyond depression, loneliness, and fear. He is the light of the world. So today, whatever your day entails, looking for the light in other people, in the changing of the seasons, in quiet, simple moments, go to the *light*.

"I will turn the darkness before them into *light*, the rough places into level ground. These are the things I will do, and I will not forsake them" (Isaiah 42:16). Have a beautiful day in the *light*!

November 15

As I sit and have my cup of coffee with Jesus, I am thinking about the word *challenge*. We live in challenging times, and every day, it seems the rules change, our energy changes, and we don't know where we're heading. But you know I love a good *challenge*, whether it is Words with Friends, a problem to solve, or better yet, the *challenge* of how to stay positive!

When I wake up every morning, the challenges are there. I put my feet on the floor, and I say, "Jesus, I give you this day, the joys, the sorrows, the challenges, and the victories. I give my life to You!" I must ignore my feelings! I just commit my life to Him. With all the challenges that we are going to face today, the most important one is staying close and committed to Jesus!

Today, don't be afraid of the challenges that face you, face them head on. Jesus is at your side each and every step of this day, and He will lead you through the challenges of *life*. Let us rejoice and be glad in it!

November 16

As I sit and have my cup of coffee with Jesus, I continued to think about the word *change*. Marcus Aurelius once said, "No man steps in the same river twice because the river has changed and so has the man." Life seems to always be in constant change, and I think we are changing too. It is the reason why a personal relationship with Christ is so important. To allow His spirit to change and mold us is to be Christlike.

I read a simple prayer that I liked, "Heavenly Father, I don't know what the future holds, but I know You hold the future." As we begin our day and go to work or school, let's embrace the change! The Spirit of God is guiding us. His Spirit reminds us that He is in control and that everything that is changing is part of this plan. *Go with the flow*!

Today, put a smile on your face and look at a beautiful new fall day in November. It's a new day and a new opportunity to make Christ present.

November 17

As I sit and have my cup of coffee with Jesus, I was thinking about *grief*. As the holidays approach, those who have dealt with the loss of a loved one sometimes experience deep *grief*. In my own life, I was thinking of the *thanksgivings* that we had when my mother and father and sister and brother were all here. Though it will never be the same, I cherish those memories, and I continue to try and celebrate the holidays.

I read a quote about grief, "In *grief* I've learned, it's really just *love*. It's all the love you want to give but cannot. All the unspent love gathers up in the corners of your eyes, a lump in your throat, and in that hollow part of your chest. Grief is just love with no place to go." But our world needs that love that we hold inside. We need to turn that love around and give it out to our families, the poor, the lonely. Then that love which we have for family members and friends continues to flow with our tears.

As we approach the holiday season, let's look at the grief in our own lives and find a way to share it with others. Have a blessed day and feel the spirit of those we miss; pay it forward, for they are just around the corner!

November 18

As I sit and have my cup of coffee with Jesus, I think of the word *perseverance*. When we turn to Jesus in times of struggle, we grow strong in perseverance. The scriptures tell us in Romans 5:3–5 that we are to "exult in our tribulations, knowing that tribulation brings about perseverance; and perseverance, proven character; and proven character hope; and hope does not disappoint, because the love of God has been poured out within our hearts through the Holy Spirit who has been given to us."

When I was a child, I remember watching TV, and suddenly, a symbol would come on and you would hear the words, "This is a test. This is only a test." The same is true with our world. When will we turn to Jesus and surrender? When will we realize how, as a world, we have turned away from Him? Today is a day to persevere. This, too, shall pass; Jesus is in control!

So today, relax, smile, it's a wonderful day. "It is just a test, it is only a test," and our faith, hope, and love are in Jesus! Have a blessed day!

November 19

As I sit and have my cup of coffee with Jesus, I was thinking about *hanging on*. Sometimes, it feels as though we're just *hanging on*. The big question becomes what are we hanging on to? Are we hanging on to the past? Are we hanging on to what the future might hold? Are we hanging on by a thread?

When times and situations seem difficult, maybe we are struggling with one of our children or grief, depression, or anxiety, we *feel* like we're *barely* hanging on. But when we have Jesus in our lives, we're not hanging on, He is *holding us up*. These all become lessons of our trust in Him and in His Word!

So today, instead of hanging on, *feel* His arms wrapped around you, feel the strength, the love, and the peace. Whatever is going on in your life, He is allowing it for your growth and holiness and for the growth and holiness of others.

Today, He is there for you, and He has His arms tightly wrapped around you. Have a blessed day, and if you're going to hang on to something, hang on to the promise that it's going to be a better day!

November 20

As I sit and have my cup of coffee with Jesus, I was thinking how God *made* this day, but it's up to us *what to make of it*! God has given us twenty-four hours, and taking away sleep, transportation, and eating, and the rest is what we *make* of it. We can wake up and dedicate our day to God, put a smile on our faces, and bring some *joy*, or we can grumble, complain, and bring people down.

If all we had left in the world were these twenty-four hours, what would we do? Don't forget, you have to be in by ten o'clock (I love rules). *Laugh*. Don't sweat the small stuff. Look for the miracles that He is doing every moment. Take a deep breath, go for a walk, call a friend…make a difference!

There are no laws or ordinances that can take away our ability to make this the *best* day ever. Have a great day, and *make* something out of it!

November 21

As I sit and have my cup of coffee with Jesus on this morning, I am thinking about *worry*! It is so easy to become worried and upset about many things. In the Bible, Luke 10:41, we hear, "Martha, Martha," and the Lord answered, "You are worried and upset about many things, but few things are needed—or indeed only one!"

People can spend the entire day worried about something, but what we really need is to spend time trusting Jesus. Jesus tells us to focus on Him. We need to open our minds to the reality that everything is in God's hand! When we worry, we cannot experience His presence in the sunrise, in our family, in the work we are to do. We are usually worried about things that have not happened yet!

So today, let us pray that we stay focused on our relationship with Jesus, knowing that we are part of His perfect plan. Let us remember that it's not our place to understand what's going on but to trust in Him. What do we have to worry about when we are a *child of* God?

Have a blessed day!

November 22

As I sit and have my cup of coffee with Jesus, I was thinking about Thanksgiving. This year, I want to prepare for it differently. There are a lot of things that we can complain about every year, but during this time of Thanksgiving, it is truly a time to search out *gratitude*.

Today, I am starting a *list* of all the things, people, and situations that I am *grateful* for. I'm going to do, showing God that I have a thankful heart even during chaos, sadness, and loss. Gratitude can certainly change our attitude. What are you grateful for? Write it down, place it in your heart, and prepare for a day of *thanksgiving* to God. No matter what has happened in our lives, as Christians, we are called to find the light in the darkness.

So start a list today; keep it with you and keep writing. It is said that the unthankful heart discovers no mercies. We need mercy! So let's begin the *vigil* of gratitude. I'm grateful that many of you connect with me each morning with my cup of coffee with Jesus, *and so is* He!

November 23

As I sit and have my cup of coffee with Jesus, I continue reflecting about Thanksgiving. Yesterday, I encouraged you to make a list of things that you're *grateful* for. Today, I want to look at the word *thanksgiving*. The words join together for thanks and giving. Gratitude and action go together. When we are truly grateful, we can't help but give of *ourselves*. That is what Jesus did, and that is what He calls us to do.

Each day, we need to look at our lives and give thanks, and not just one day a year. Along with giving thanks, we need to move into *action*, and that is the *giving* part, giving of our time, talents, and treasures, each giving according to our gratitude. Everything we have and are comes from the Father, and we are held accountable.

So today, make a list of the *giving*, the *time, talent,* and *treasure* that you are going to *share* with our world, a world that is in desperate need. Can you imagine what kind of world we would live in if we all gave thanks and shared our gifts? Have a blessed day!

November 24

As I sit and have my cup of coffee with Jesus during this beautiful Thanksgiving season, it is all about *gratitude*. In the last few days, I shared about making a list of things you're grateful for. I shared about action for thanks always leads to giving (*thanksgiving*), and today, it's adding it all up. No matter how difficult the years may be, God has been *faithful* and blessed us. There is nowhere in the Bible that it says that life will be easy!

Jesus says, "Come to me, all you who labor and are burdened, and I will give you rest. Take my yoke upon you and learn from me, I am meek and humble of heart; and you will find rest for yourselves. For my yoke is easy, and my burden light."

So during this season, bring your fears, pains, sorrows, trials, and tribulations, and lift them up to the cross and *praise* God. Focus on the light of Christ, not on the darkness, and you will find that you have a lot to be *grateful* for. This, too, *shall* pass, and we will experience, as a world and a nation, and in our personal lives, Emmanuel—God *is with us*! No matter how we celebrate Thanksgiving, what is most important is that we give *thanks*. Feel free to have a piece of pie before your meal in memory of my mother…it's a great family tradition.

And thank you for being a friend and journeying with me in a complete surrender to our Lord!

November 25

As I sit and have my cup of coffee with Jesus, I watch as the sun comes up; it is the beginning of a new day. A new day can mean many things. It can mean worrying about problems and dreading getting certain things done, or it can be filled with *excitement* and *adventure*. A new day can be filled with depression and sadness, or it can be seen as a new opportunity for *joy* and *peace*.

Our lives are full of *choices*, and each *choice* has a consequence. Today, we can choose to make this day the Lord's Day. *We can move from stressed to blessed!* We can choose to surrender our problems and worries to Him. We can choose to make this a wonderful day! That is one of the greatest gifts that God has given us, the gift to *choose*.

Today, let's *choose* to fill our day with God's awesome love and peace. This is our day to *give* back to Him gratitude, love, and *joy*!

November 26

As I sit and have my cup of coffee with Jesus, I was thinking about a quote a friend shared from C. S. Lewis. "You don't have a soul. You are a soul. You have a body." Sometimes, I think we need to *reclaim* our souls. Our soul is the God that lives within us, always available to us, and that place where we can find *peace* and *joy*.

Our bodies are temporary, they house our souls for a period of time until our souls are set free. We get attached to our bodies or to the bodies of people we love, and that's why grief can be so difficult. It is easy to reclaim the *soul*. Step back into silence, take a deep breath, and go to that inner space where God dwells!

God waits patiently for us to be *one* with Him!

Today, instead of getting caught up in the regular daily rush, take just a few moments and let your *soul* connect to God. You'll find your purpose and meaning in the peace and joy you seek. Have a blessed day and the soul connection!

November 27

As I sit and have my cup of coffee with Jesus, I am thinking about something that Saint Teresa of Avila once said, "Let nothing disturb you, let nothing frighten you. Though all things pass, God does not change. Patience wins all things! But he lacks nothing who possesses God; for God alone suffices!"

As we approach Advent, we are preparing for the *light* of Christ to come into our world. What perfect timing. When it seems that the world is so dark, with *joy* and *anticipation*, we can welcome the light.

The darkness, too, will pass, as it has generation after generation, but we must search for the *light*. Today is a great day to think ahead, to think of this Advent season in which we can spiritually prepare for the *light*, welcoming Jesus into our world, our nation, our families, and our hearts!

Let's not stay in the darkness, let's embrace the *light*!

November 28

As I sit and have my cup of coffee with Jesus, I am excited to begin preparation of Christmas. Today, I will begin putting out decorations for a season that brings Jesus present in a unique way. I am going to bring that energy to life.

I'll be putting out Christmas lights to brighten up this world. I'll be putting up a tree and decorating it. I'll be getting my Advent wreath ready for four weeks of anticipation and excitement, preparing for Jesus's coming! I will set up a Nativity scene (but no Jesus in it yet) to remind me of the journey and story. I will unpack my mother's favorite decoration, a bowl made from peppermints made by my grandmother! I will begin playing Christmas music and enjoying the scriptures of the season.

This year, I will do everything I can to bring the true spirit of Christmas to myself and to everyone I encounter. We need Jesus. We need Jesus now more than ever. We need the light of Christ to shine on our world! What a great day to get ready, because ready or not, *here* He *comes*!

November 29

As I sit and have my cup of coffee with Jesus, I lit my first Advent candle representing *hope*. Can you think of anything greater that our world needs right now than *hope*? Can you also imagine if each person opened their heart to God's Spirit, how *hope* would be fulfilled?

Today, you have that opportunity to bring *hope*. Every time you go outside yourself and do something selfless, you bring *hope*! Every time you show an act of love, you bring *hope*. From a simple smile to bringing food for the poor, every act of love brings *hope*. When you trust God with your worries and anxieties, that brings *hope*. When you surrender and put your trust in Him, it brings *hope*!

So today, get in the spirit of the anticipation and preparation of Jesus Christ coming into our world. Light your candle, and be a sign of *hope* to our world.

November 30

As I sit and have my cup of coffee with Jesus, I was thinking of how important the Advent season is. It is a time for us to remember that we can't always *figure* out everything we are called to *live*, to journey. Advent takes us on a journey to Christ.

Many times, we spend or waste so much time trying to *figure* things out instead of living in the present moment in His presence! We cannot always figure out why some people suffer or are sick or why our plans don't always turn out as we want. There are many aspects of life that I don't understand. I just have to *trust* that they are in my life for a reason. I must *trust* Jesus! So get out of your head and into your heart and today in Him.

We are children of God, *beloved* by God, on a journey to know Him, love Him, and serve Him! I may not be able to figure it all out or understand it all, I just need to *trust* it. Have a blessed day!

December 1

As I sit and have my cup of coffee with Jesus, I find it hard to believe it's already December! I am finding myself needing to force myself to get into the Christmas season. I'm a visual person, so my house is already set up. I'm putting all my energy into the *spiritual* preparation.

I have my regular devotionals that I read every day, and of course, the Office (prayer of the church), and the rosary. I know that I need more to bring the season to my heart. So this Advent, I am making a special prayer list to be prayed by name every day for those seeking prayer for illness, struggles, addictions, or whatever they need in prayer. This is something you can do too, and each morning, I am going to read their names out loud.

If you have a prayer request, please feel free to respond to me with it, and I will add it to my list. Advent is a time to welcome Jesus, to renew our faith in Him, and to bring His light to the world. What better way than with prayer!

Today, make a list, and let's pray for our world, our families, and for all those needing prayer!

December 2

As I sit and have my cup of coffee with Jesus, I was thinking about *brokenness*. During the holiday season, it is a time I think about my family and those I have lost. I have become very aware of my own *brokenness and loss*.

I think one of the things that connects us as human beings is our own *brokenness*. Our brokenness tells us something about ourselves.

Your brokenness tells me something about you and mine about me.

I don't know if one person's suffering is greater than another's. *Suffering* is such a personal thing, but when we connect our brokenness, something very real happens.

The greatest brokenness is our separation in relationships. We need to embrace our brokenness, to name it, and then, the most painful part, see it as a gift. The last couple of years, I feel like the vase that has been shattered into a million pieces.

When I search for the silver lining, I see how many other broken people have come to me. We share stories and tears, and that is not easy. I could write books on *brokenness*. At times, I feel lonely, disconnected, scared, and very vulnerable, and that is when God brings amazing people who share their *brokenness*. This Advent season, I light my candle for all those who know what it means to be *broken* but to have faith. This is why Jesus came into the world.

Today, I lift up all those who feel *broken*. You are not alone.

And *we* are the reason that Jesus came! Have a blessed day as Jesus sends His healing!

I can't wait to see what Jesus will make out of all the broken pieces I call me.

December 3

As I sit and have my cup of coffee with Jesus, I was thinking about all the responses yesterday about *brokenness*. A few friends came by, and we shared our own brokenness. One shared about a disconnect from a child, one shared about the fear they are experiencing with the chaos in the world, and I talked about the despair that happens when your life gets turned upside down.

The beauty of our discussion was that we could all be vulnerable. We realize that each of our pain differs in some ways; it is really just pain.

We talked about the *healing* needed in our lives. Henri Nouwen says, "The first step to healing is not a step away from the pain, but a step toward it." I like this quote, but it is easier said than done. He challenges us to think of one kind of brokenness in our life that we have avoided rather than befriended.

Today, with the help of Jesus, I'm going to strive to embrace the brokenness, the pain, the abandonment, and *trust* in His healing *grace*. Brokenness does not make us victims unless we allow it. One of my favorite actions in the Mass is when the priest takes the Eucharist and breaks it. It reminds me of our oneness with Jesus and His brokenness. Today is going to be a great day because I am not alone in my brokenness! I have our Lord and so do you!

Have a beautiful day!

December 4

As I sit and have my cup of coffee with Jesus, I have been thinking about the chapters I'm reading in Henri Nouwen's book, *Life of the Beloved*. He speaks a lot about brokenness, but he also speaks about *blessing*.

He says, "To give someone a blessing is the most significant affirmation we can offer." Whether we ask the Lord to bless our children as they leave the house, bless those who persecuted you (that's a hard one), or when you're driving down the street and you see a homeless person, to share a blessing. It is bringing the Christ in you to others.

Today I'm going to strive to *bless* our world, one person at a time. I'm going to ask Jesus to touch their hearts, to fill them with *peace*, to *heal* their brokenness, and to bless them this day.

Have a blessed day!

December 5

As I sit and have my cup of coffee with Jesus, I continued to reflect on the wisdom of Henri Nouwen in his book *Life of the Beloved*. As much as he talks about brokenness, Nouwen also reflects on *blessings*. The blessings that come through brokenness, though it is not always easy to see your blessings when you feel attacked, depressed, and hurt. But the blessings are everywhere!

The *blessings* begin with waking up in the morning, and forgetting your feelings, know that this *new* day is a *blessing*! To thank God that we live in a home, have family that cares about us, food to eat—these are all basic blessings. But we must go deeper. The Spirit moves us to see that even our trials are blessings, as they draw us closer to Jesus. God brings Simons, like Simon of Cyrene, to walk with us and to help us carry our crosses. If we open our eyes, we see that everything is changing, and *everything* is a *blessing*!

Today I'm counting my blessings, praying for those who find it difficult to get out of bed and wonder what their purpose is. Our purpose today is to *live*, to know, love, and serve our God. What a blessing today is!

Have a blessed day!

December 6

As I sit and have my cup of coffee with Jesus, I was reflecting on the promises of Jesus! Do you feel sometimes that God is not hearing your prayers? The questions are real, but Jesus reminds us that he fulfills all his promises. He has saved us!

Sometimes, we feel like giving up; sometimes, we feel the attacks are more than we can handle. Jesus reminded St. Paul, "My grace is sufficient for you, for my power is made perfect in weakness!"

It's all about surrendering, praying, and trusting. A wonderful daily prayer is the Surrender Novena, "O Jesus, I surrender myself to you, you take care of everything!" What a great time to be with the Lord, to pray, to *slow down, simplify,* and *sanctify*!

Have a blessed day!

December 7

As I sit and have my cup of coffee with Jesus, I was thinking of a quote a friend sent yesterday. It says, "*Optimist*: someone who figures that taking a step backward after taking a step forward is not a disaster, it's a cha-cha." That really made me smile!

We must strive to be *optimists* during this time to see the *light*. That is what the Advent season is all about. Maybe you feel like me; you feel you move forward and then you get knocked back a few steps. We must pick ourselves up, *trust* in Jesus, and maybe instead of complaining, we just need to *dance*.

Every once in a while, if I was having a bad day, my mother would turn on the music in the kitchen and grab my arms, and we would dance. And before long, I forgot what I was upset about. I think today I'm going to have to start dancing. Have a blessed day, put a smile on your face, and be an *optimist*. We can all make this a better world by allowing the Holy Spirit to make hearts dance with *joy*.

Though my mother has passed, I think I hear her, "Come on, Craig, let's dance."

December 8

As I sit and have my cup of coffee with Jesus, I couldn't help but think about the *pain* in the world today. People grieving the loss of loved ones, *pain* in relationships, failed love, separation from family members, unhealed hurts. But pain always leads to something *greater*!

Like a mother in labor, the pain is intense until she holds the new life entrusted to her. Like the gold medalists who didn't earn their medals without working through pain. Every marriage that I have ever seen had to work through pain to enjoy a life with family and love. It's so easy to want to *run* from the pain or numb the pain; Jesus's example on the cross tells us to *embrace* the pain.

Today, I will see God's *perfect* plan working even in the pain. I will draw closer to Him and ask for the strength to grow strong! Today, we can embrace whatever struggles we have and know that God is working out His perfect plan. We can pick up our cross, or sometimes crosses, and trust in His plan. We don't need to not focus on the pain, but on the *promise*!

Have a blessed day!

December 9

As I sit and have my cup of coffee with Jesus, I'm reflecting on God's *will*. There are times it is very clear to me, and other times I wrestle with my own will. Many times, it takes me out of my comfort zone. My morning prayer time is my time to center on what God wants me to do. Sometimes, God is very clear, and sometimes, I must just *trust*.

What is powerful for me is the special time in the morning where I listen to God, and I know God listens to me (and laughs). Every day, it's important for us to remember to spend time with God. Even though God may take you through a journey you never expected, you will not feel alone. A friend sent me a quote yesterday, "Sometimes, faith will make you look stupid, until it rains." (Noah!)

Today, I am going to focus on this beautiful Advent season. I'm going to remember what this is about—Jesus! I'm not going to worry about the flood. I'm just going to serve our Lord, even when it is outside my comfort zone.

Have a blessed day!

December 10

As I sit and have my cup of coffee with Jesus, I was reflecting on WALKING in faith. It's hard to know what to believe today. What is real news, what is fake news, what are the laws and the rules that seem to change every day. But what I do know is we need to WALK in faith, and the only news we should trust is the GOOD NEWS of Jesus Christ.

To WALK in faith means to TRUST in God's word and HIS promises, HIS Commandments. It means being true to SELF but allowing the Spirit of God to direct your life. How blessed we are that our CREATOR fills us with HIS SPIRIT to be our guide. If we're sad, depressed, or going through a trial, or struggling, we just need to go to HIS WORD (The GOOD NEWS) and HIS promises. We may live in confusing times, but God is never confusing.

So, today open the GOOD NEWS of Jesus Christ and listen to the TRUTH and follow HIS guidance. In the end, nothing else matters but to be true to self and true to God. Jesus, I surrender myself to You. Take care of everything!

Have a blessed day!

December 11

As I sit and have my cup of coffee with Jesus and light my second Advent candle, I realize how much I need the *light*. As a child, I fought depression and continue to do so today. As the winter comes and the sun goes away, I can always feel it coming on, and with everything around me, there's a *deep* darkness. But I cannot allow myself to be in darkness, and so I constantly must reach out to the *light* of Christ!

I try to surround myself with good people who are positive, I read positive books, I love the positive quotes, and sometimes, humor that people send to me. I try to stay away from the darkness, but the only true way is to continue to invite Jesus into the darkness. The scriptures help me to reflect on the *light*.

Today was one of those days. I woke up sad and dark, and yet Jesus comes to me and *lifts* me up. He dispels the darkness and reminds me that all is in His hands. Today, more than ever, I will embrace the light.

I am living in His presence.

Have a blessed day in His light!

December 12

As I sit and have my cup of coffee with Jesus on this beautiful morning, the day we honor our Lady of Guadalupe, I think of my mother, as today is her birthday. Yesterday brought the realization to me that I need to work harder at seeing the *presence* of God in everything. I lit my second candle on my Advent wreath, and the light is very bright!

There are times we go up and down and even sideways, but the consistent factor in our life must be Jesus Christ! As my coffee mug says, Matthew 28:20, "I am with you always." It is the perfect reminder we are never alone. It also reminds me that it's the little thoughtful things that people do that spreads the love of Christ. The oranges left at my front door, the beautiful Christmas cards I receive, a visit from a longtime friend, all create blessings. All the simple things remind me of how blessed I am.

Today is my turn to show kindness, to be the light to others, and to celebrate that Jesus is with us always. Just like my car battery yesterday, everything and everyone sometimes just needs a boost.

Have a blessed day!

December 13

As I sit and have my cup of coffee with Jesus and light the third candle on my Advent wreath (rose), I am reflecting on the word *joy*. I have come to believe that we do not just have *joy*, we need to search it out. There is a difference between happiness and joy.

I was corrected one day by an eight-year-old who told me I did not understand the word *joy*. I asked him "What does it mean?"

And he said, "It's just how it's spelled. The J is for Jesus, the O is for others, and the Y is for you."

Joy! He was right, and when you put it in the right order, you experience peace, contentment, oneness, wholeness, and enlightenment. You can even experience *joy* when you're in pain or suffering.

So today, I'm going to stop experiencing Y (you first), O (others second), and J (Jesus last), and *enjoy* this new day, putting Jesus first, then others, and then myself.

Have a great and blessed day!

December 14

As I sit and have my cup of coffee with Jesus, I was reflecting on a conversation with a friend of mine yesterday. He said, "There's just no *spirit* in Christmas this year!" I agreed with him, but then last night, I was thinking about it. The Spirit of Jesus is *in* us, and if we are not trusting Him and allowing the Spirit to come forth, there is no real reason to celebrate Christmas.

The holiday originated to honor the newborn king, Emmanuel, "God is with us," to pray, to sing, to worship, and to *welcome* Jesus. Then it became commercialized. Just maybe we need to look back at the *real* meaning of Christmas, so parties may be canceled, gifts may be simplified, and many of us may even spend Christmas alone. But we do have the choice to spend it with Jesus.

Today, we can begin to bring that Spirit of Jesus alive with our words, our attitudes, our *kindness*, and our excitement; this is what the season is truly about. The next days can be filled with sadness and complaining, or it can be filled with Jesus. It's our choice!

Let's prepare to welcome the newborn, care, and get into the *spirit*!

December 15

As I sit and have my cup of coffee with Jesus and the three candles on my Advent wreath are lit, I'm reflecting on *connections*. The Advent season and Christmas are certainly about Jesus, but it is also a time of connections, the *connection* between God and humankind, the connection that God wishes us to have with His Son, and the connection that God desires us to have with each other.

One of the gifts of the season is the gift of Christmas cards, a simple gift of *connection*. I love looking at how families have grown. I love seeing the way people age gracefully. I love to know someone is thinking of me, and it makes me think of them. Connection is a *gift* from God!

So today, even if you don't feel like connecting, reach out, send out a few cards letting people know that you are thinking of them. It's much more personal than a text! Today, have a blessed day and connect; when we connect with each other, we connect to Jesus, and when we connect to Jesus, we find the Father.

December 16

As I sit and have my cup of coffee with Jesus, I was thinking about the word PEACE! It really is an amazing word. We can use it to describe inner peace, peace in the family, peace in our world. Jesus is called the Prince of PEACE! I think that before we can strive for peace in our world it has to begin in our own hearts.

The world has been forced to slow down. If we can take a deep breath and be present in the moment, we can find HIS PEACE. If we don't look at the past, and don't worry about the future, but live in the present, in HIS presence, we can find peace!

Today, I'm going to be aware of my breath, I'm going to take time to look at the changing season, I'm going to become aware that even in the chaos I can find peace. Jesus said, "My PEACE I leave you; My peace I give you. I do not give to you as the world gives, do not let your hearts be troubled and do not be afraid." John 14:27. If we can find that PEACE, then we can pass it on...

Have a PEACE filled day!

December 17

As I sit and have my cup of coffee with Jesus, I'm reflecting on the word *journey*! During Advent, we journey with Mary and Joseph and the Magi following the *star*! On most journeys, sometimes, we look back and we see how far we have come, and sometimes, we get anxious and look ahead to see how far we still must go.

I remember, as a child, going on a trip, we would pull out a big folded map and mark our trips. The line drawn on the map made it seem we didn't have far to go, but some of those trips felt like a lifetime sitting in the station wagon with my siblings. The signs on the road kept changing, but all I knew for sure was we were moving forward. Our life is a journey, and we move forward to the promises of Christ given to us in the Bible, a *life* with no more tears, no more sadness, an eternal life in the *presence* of our Lord!

Today, my journey begins by opening my *heart* to the Lord, letting Him show me on the map where He wants me to go. Today,

I am trusting Him that it's His map I must follow…His plan. Today is a great adventure, a great journey, because each day, we get closer to Him!

Have a great journey today, and don't forget His map!

December 18

As I sit and have my cup of coffee with Jesus, I was thinking about the gift of FRIENDSHIP. You come to know who your real friends are when you go through tough times in life. It's painful, sometimes, when friendships change or end. Christmas is a time of renewing friendships. Last night, as I sat by my fireplace and I looked at Christmas cards, I realized I am blessed with friends.

But I also thought about what kind of friend I am. Do I reach out to people when they are suffering, sick, troubled? Am I a true friend or is it just when it is convenient? True friends are hard to come by, but when you find one, it's like finding a rare pearl. Jesus desires to be our friend, someone we can trust! Jesus is there for us to share our fears and trials, knowing that HE will stand by us.

Today I'm going to pray in a special way for my friends (even my four-legged ones) and that I can be a good friend. And I'm going to thank God for the gift of friendships, true friendships. I'm going to reach out to a friend who may be in need today!

Have a blessed day!

December 19

As I sit and have my cup of coffee with Jesus (and Baileys!), I was thinking about *traditions*. I think every family has traditions that have been passed down for the Christmas season. One family shared how they decorate their tree in one night, bringing out all the ornaments one by one, remembering where they came from and who gave it to them.

Another family shared how they gather to make tamales, another ravioli. And then there are these awesome Polish cookies. Traditions are important; they remind us of our past and our heritage. They make us remember those people who passed them down, and that we are people on a journey.

Today, think about the traditions that you celebrated over the years to welcome Jesus into the world. Christmas is about memories, families, and traditions that remind us that Jesus is our *king*! Don't forget to drop off some of those traditions on my porch!

Have a blessed day!

December 20

As I sit and have my cup of coffee with Jesus, I'm thinking about the fourth candle of Advent. The final candle represents the angels coming to declare the birth of the newborn King!

Perhaps Jesus knows we need a sign that everything is going to be okay, a reminder that Jesus came into the world, and that maybe He will get our attention! It's not too late to save our world. I am lighting my candle with faith and hope in Jesus.

Tomorrow, I will be remembering that I am not alone, that the light of Jesus is always with me!

Have a great day!

December 21

As I sit and have my cup of coffee with Jesus again, I am excited about the *star*, the light of Christ. Matthew 2:9–10 says, "They went on their way, and the star they had seen in the East went ahead of them until it stopped over the place where the child was. When they saw the star, they were *overjoyed*."

Maybe this is a way God will get our attention as he did two thousand years ago. The star led them to Christ, and now we are called to be *living stars*, leading others to Christ! Just for one day, I hope the world looks beyond all the problems and separation and gazes upward, acknowledging Jesus Christ, *our King*!

Happy stargazing!

December 22

As I sit and have my cup of coffee with Jesus, I was thinking again about the *star* that the shepherds followed. I thought of the immensity and greatness of God compared to the "thick and dreadful darkness" that some people experience. If you know that "dreadful darkness," you know what I'm talking about. It is that separation from all that makes us feel that way. I am reminded of how great God is that when we reach beyond our own thoughts, we can connect with the universe out there and *to the* Creator!

There were all kinds of problems during Jesus's time, some political and economic; there was sickness and death, and to this, Jesus came to bring the promises and the *light* of God. Only a couple days left to welcome the newborn King, the *one* who can take us out of that "thick and dreadful darkness" and bring us to light! Turn to the light, welcome the light, live in the light!

Have a blessed day!

December 23

As I sit and have my cup of coffee with Jesus, I was thinking about *gifts*. My gifts for my family are all wrapped and under the tree, but I am thinking about the *greater* gifts. What gifts have I received this year? I received the gift of *patience*. Waiting and waiting for direction has shown me patience. I received the gift of *perseverance*, even when I felt like giving up. I received the gift of *friendship* from many around me. I received the gift of *tears* through personal losses. I received the gift of *healing* as Jesus works deeper in my life. I received the gift of *forgiveness* as I strive to forgive those in my life I need to forgive.

Even though I received a lot of gifts, what gift am I giving Jesus for His birthday since this is all about Him? What could I possibly give Him? The only thing I can give Him completely is *myself*. I can give Him my loneliness, my *brokenness*, my fears. These are the only true gifts I can give Him. It doesn't seem much to give the King of kings, but it's all I need to *give*!

What are you going to give Jesus this Christmas?

December 24

As I sit and have my cup of coffee with Jesus on Christmas Eve morning, I think about why Jesus came into the world. The incarnation is about *change*! When humankind lost its vision of the Creator, God visited us on earth. His name was Jesus, and He came to bring change.

Jesus came to proclaim Good News! He came to heal and bring us back into relationship with the Father. He comes again to bring *change*, to remind our world that we were created to *love*. He came to remind the world today that we need to get rid of all bitterness and hate, judgment and condemnation. He came to remind us to care for the least of us!

Today, I am going to reflect on what I need to change in my life. *Change* begins with reflection, and reflection with gratitude. I realize how powerfully God has worked in my life! I acknowledge this, and I'm grateful for His love and guidance, even through the most difficult times of life! Today, I welcome Jesus into my life, my heart, our world. Emmanuel God *is with us*!

I think I will sing all day!

December 25

As I sit and have my cup of coffee with Jesus, I celebrate Emmanuel, God is with us! I am grateful for all that Jesus has done in my life, and I welcome Him into this season of love, joy, and *peace*.

Today, we celebrate, we remember, and we renew our relationship with Jesus Christ. No matter what trials and tribulations, no matter what hardships and suffering have passed through *our* doors, Jesus has never left us, and He promises us He never will. So today as we celebrate His birth, let us thank the Father for sending Him to us to save us, to redeem us, and to unite us with our Creator!

Thank you for the outpouring of love, cards, gifts, and texts, reminding me of the love that can only come from Jesus. We don't need to look back, and we don't need to look to the future today. Let us live in the *present* moment and in His presence and celebrate the gift of the newborn King.

Merry Christmas and a blessed New Year!

December 26

As I sit and have my cup of coffee with Jesus, I can only be filled with *gratitude*, gratitude for the entire Advent and Christmas season. It was centered on Jesus; His presence was so powerful. From taking the dog for a walk, to the quiet time to reading Christmas cards, and dinner with friends, I found peace. I even watched an old Christmas movie!

At dinner, we were talking about Christmases past. We shared all the activities and memories of when we were children. It made us realize how present Jesus has always been in our lives. The large gatherings, the big meals, the presents, the school performances, the office parties, all those activities were part of Christ's plan for us.

So today is a Day of Gratitude for reminding me of how blessed I have been and what sometimes I took for granted. Thank you, Lord, for a *true* Christmas. By the way, Christmas is not over; we continue to celebrate the *presence* of Jesus in our world.

December 27

As I sit and have my cup of coffee with Jesus on this beautiful day, I am celebrating the feast of the Holy Family. I can't help but think about *family* at this time of the year. We have biological families, we have adopted families and foster families, and we have those special people we call family. Today, I give thanks to God for all the families who have been a part of my life. I remember those family members who have already passed, and I thank God for the gifts they shared with me in this life.

What makes a family holy is its desire to stay together. This requires *forgiveness*, *love*, and *mercy* time and time again. I've never met a family that did not have issues, but if they had love, I knew they could work through anything. Today is a great day to remember that we need to *forgive*! If there is somebody in your family who has hurt you, has caused dissension in the family, who struggles with addiction or mental illness, today, *forgive*. Turn to God, mention them by name, and ask God to give you the grace to *forgive*. That does not mean that you don't need to have boundaries or that problems will disappear. It just means you have given it to God.

Today, we honor the Holy Family by showing love to our own family, by loving them, by forgiving them! May you be blessed, and may Jesus bless all our families. And to my family, thank you for loving me!

December 28

As I sit and have my cup of coffee with Jesus, I see that a couple of my neighbors already have their Christmas trees out on the curb. I want to tell them that Christmas is not over yet, that the Christmas season ends with the Epiphany. So we need to change our thinking about Christmas; it is not over, it has really just begun. It is easy to fall into the idea of a secular Christmas where it's all about the presents and the parties and then, finally to say, "I'm glad it's over." That is no way to welcome the birth of Christ. The celebration needs to continue.

The tree may be dry and some of the lights burned out, but it's time to reflect on the Nativity. The hoopla is over; now it is time to get into the true spirit of Christmas.

Today, we need to start thinking about the new year, how we are going to bring positive energy, joy, peace, and love into the world, and how we are going to *refocus*, *reconnect*, and *renew*!

Have a blessed day!

December 29

As I sit and have my cup of coffee with Jesus, I am continuing to prepare for the beginning of the new year. I have never really believed in resolutions as much as in setting some goals. I try to think of things that I want to improve emotionally, spiritually, mentally, and physically. I think of books that I would like to read, classes I'd like to take, spiritual exercises to practice, eating more healthfully, taking care of my body, looking deeper into myself, and connecting with God.

I like to write these down but not put time limits or restrictions on them. I think about and listen to where God wants to take me. I like to reflect on where I've been and where God is leading me. Whether the last year was full of challenges or blessings, it is now in the past, and we need to look forward and into the light. I believe that next year is what we will make of it as individuals, families, communities, and even the world. It's time to create the energy that will bring about change, and I believe that comes from Jesus.

Today, I will spend some time in quiet and prayer, listening to what God is asking of me. I will write these down and make them my prayer to welcome the new year. I trust that this new year will be filled with amazing possibilities, healing, justice, and peace. I will *surrender* to His will; I *will trust in* Him!

Have a blessed day!

December 30

As I sit and have my cup of coffee with Jesus, I continued to reflect on the upcoming year. We need to enter this year without *fear*, putting our *trust* in Jesus. We must challenge ourselves to begin each day with a positive attitude and to live life to the fullest. We need to bring *joy* and *peace* to this world, one person at a time.

I think the best way to do this is to have a heart full of *gratitude*, gratitude for the blessings that come, even during our trials, the blessings of endurance, perseverance, and hope. We need to turn to *prayer* for this *new year*, asking God to change our hearts.

It all begins with us individually, in *our* own hearts and actions, inviting Jesus in, renewing our relationship with Him each morning, asking Him what we can do to make things better.

It is going to be a great day and a great new year!

December 31

As I sit and have my cup of coffee with Jesus on this New Year's Eve morning, I'm finishing up my list of ways I want to challenge myself in the *new year*. I always make a list, not resolutions, a list of areas of growth. I make a goal of how I want to grow *spiritually* and build my relationship with the Lord. I make a goal of how I want to grow *emotionally*, including books I want to read, classes I'm going to take, ways in which I can grow *inwardly*. And then I set a goal for *physical* growth. I look at ways in which I can take better care of the temple God has put me in charge of.

I don't set unachievable goals; I just seek ways in which I can set patterns for the new year. I think of the healing that I need and the areas in which I need to grow in forgiveness, patience, and trust. I have come to believe that God sometimes takes us to places and gives us experiences to draw us closer to Him!

So today, I'm going to prepare prayerfully to walk into this *new year* with strength and trust that each trial and blessing, no matter how difficult, is part of God's greater plan to build His kingdom. That becomes exciting and challenging, knowing that God has taught me and continues to teach me to surrender, trust, love, and serve Him! I can't help but be excited about a *new year*!

Ready or not, here I come, with Jesus at my side.

About the Author

Craig Harrison served as an ordained minister for thirty-five years. He has a family consisting of eight adopted children and nineteen grandchildren. He is the author of the children's book, *Angel Girl*, and *Pax et Bonum*, a reflection on his many trips to Assisi, Italy, the home of St. Francis. He is an inspirational speaker and continues to work with families through grief and trauma.